No Cape Required

No Cape Required

Empowering Abundant Leadership

Bob Hughes
Helen Caton Hughes

 BUSINESS EXPERT PRESS

No Cape Required: Empowering Abundant Leadership
Copyright © Business Expert Press, LLC, 2019.

First published in 2019 by
Business Expert Press, LLC
222 East 46th Street, New York, NY 10017
www.businessexpertpress.com

ISBN-13: 978-1-94999-119-2 (paperback)
ISBN-13: 978-1-94999-120-8 (e-book)

Business Expert Press Human Resource Management and Organizational Behavior Collection

Collection ISSN: 1946-5637 (print)
Collection ISSN: 1946-5645 (electronic)

Cover and interior design by S4Carlisle Publishing Services Private Ltd., Chennai, India

First edition: 2019

10 9 8 7 6 5 4 3 2 1

Printed in the United States of America.

Dedication

To our mentors and managers: Paul Edwards, Brian Giffen,
Marc Auckland, and Mike Opie
Thank you
And to our mothers, Barbara Hughes and Irene Caton,
Words are not enough.

Advance Quotes
for *No Cape Required*

"This is a long-overdue book, challenging the dominant male hero-leader paradigm and proposing an environment of more inclusive leadership, that will deliver results in today's world of work. The authors address more than gender equality; it's about understanding that diversity and inclusion are not just vital for organisational success, but for individual wellbeing too. No engagement without inclusion! *No Cape Required* puts the issues on the table and demonstrates the Pound, Dollar and Euro value to organisations of developing more abundant leadership."

—Nita Clarke OBE,
Director, Involvement and Participation Association (IPA),
Raising performance through workforce engagement,
and co-chair, Engage for Success

"Leadership today has never been more challenging or challenged. Pace of change, the need for innovation and productivity, and ability to adapt alongside greater transparency place significant demands and require a different way of thinking. This book pushes us all towards more open, inclusive, and engaging leadership, and the idea of abundance to transform together. It is rich in insights, evidence and practical guidance, and how to think about leadership development as much as part of culture as it is a process."

—Peter Cheese,
Chief Executive, CIPD,
The professional body for HR and people development

"Organisations face growing pressures to perform, in an evermore challenging and uncertain world. It is increasingly important that everyone feels able to deliver their best contributions for the benefit of the organisation and for their own sense of wellbeing. This book demonstrates how this can be addressed; at the level of individual managers and leaders, working with their teams in inclusive, coaching and respectful ways. NO CAPE REQUIRED is an important contribution at a pivotal time for our country."

—David MacLeod OBE,
Co-author of *Engaging For Success* (the MacLeod Report, BIS 2009)

"NO CAPE REQUIRED makes a powerful case that we don't need to find the right leader for everyone . . . rather we need everyone to start being a leader. More than that, this book shows you where to start."

—David Burkus,
Author of *Friend of A Friend* and *Under New Management*

"We're living in a VUCA World already and I'm pleased to see that NO CAPE REQUIRED focuses on the kind of leaders we need in this volatile, uncertain, complex and ambiguous environment.

Readers can take away thought provoking ideas for developing better individual leadership and creating a positive climate for thriving organisations in our VUCA World."

—Stephen Dando,
Operating Partner, Bain Capital

"*No Cape Required* is a liberating read for HR professionals, OD practitioners and managers generally, as it demonstrates something that we inherently know. Leadership is not about position in a hierarchy. It is about having the desire to make a difference and having the skills to reach out to others to involve them in making the change. The difficulty has always been where do people who want to make this contribution start if they don't have the trappings of office or if they feel they want to make a greater impact. *No Cape Required* gives you some important insights into starting or accelerating your journey and the journey of those around you.

This is an important and worthwhile read for all of us."

—Geoff Lloyd,
CHRO, Meggitt PLC

Abstract

No Cape Required: Empowering Abundant Leadership sets out a vision for a new approach to leadership and emphasizes the need to develop both the individual and the organizational environment within which he or she is expected to lead and succeed.

This book illumines the path toward taking leadership development into your own hands and influencing the organization around you to be better prepared for the abundant leadership revolution.

You will learn how costly is the dominant hero-leader paradigm and why it's vital, in today's "VUCA World" of volatility, uncertainty, complexity, and ambiguity, to develop a new and more relevant approach to leadership and leadership development.

If you are a manager yourself, this book offers insight into the behaviors and skills you need to deliver and the engaging styles you can use to build more successful teams and experience better relationships with colleagues.

This book addresses equality through its message of abundant leadership; not emphasizing one group over another, but pointing out the need to unlock the talents and potential of everyone in the organization.

Keywords

abundant leadership; leadership development; organizational development; VUCA; volatility; uncertainty; complexity; ambiguity; change; transformation; coaching style; leadership; management

Contents

Acknowledgments

Thanks are due to many people who've supported us in writing and preparing this book for publication. To our many clients, who've applied their own leadership coaching skills to help us meet our publishing goals.

To Dr. Janine Brooks MBE and Joan Reid, Career Coach, for reviewing the book.

To Alan Sears, Head Honcho at Vybrant, for suggesting the "Leadership by Lion Taming" metaphor.

To our dear colleagues, around the world, who—each in their own way—have contributed their experience and wisdom to bring this book into the world, especially to Cynthia Calluori, at CCA, Toronto, Canada, and Tony Draper in Brisbane, Australia—both fine leadership coaches who continually challenge us to think more, feel more, and achieve more.

Thank you.

Helen Caton Hughes
Bob Hughes
May 2018

Find out more

To find out more about Forton Leadership and Coaching, the My360 leadership diagnostic tool, or Bob and Helen's work, go to

www.thefortongroup.com or contact info@thefortongroup.com

Introduction

Our strength is in a system, not heroes. A heroic, high-minded system.
—Eric Garland

There's a book on leadership written every 6 minutes, so they say. And you can see why. Everyone's got an opinion on the subject—those who lead, as well as those who are led. Because we've all got bosses; we've all experienced the highs and lows. Yet few of us have experienced good leadership. This book is about developing better leadership. It's about redefining the very term *leadership*. And it's about drawing upon, and growing, everyone's abundant leadership capabilities.

In the 25 years we've been supporting leaders to grow, develop, and deliver, we've seen all the fads:

- It's all about traits—"leaders are born."
- It's all about character—"leaders are made."
- It's hero leadership.
- It's servant leadership.
- It's these leadership styles. *No—it's these . . .*

With a few noble exceptions, the hero leader model perpetuates its "solo male and stale leader" stereotype—complete with cape. These people are bosses, not necessarily leaders. Yes, these people have status, hovering at the top of their organizations. But the price they pay is isolation and loneliness, and, knowingly or otherwise, they suppress the value locked up in their organizations. They're trapped by their own status. And it creates an artificially narrow barrier to entry for others. It's a monoculture; where diversity, strengths, and contribution are undervalued in favor of adherence to an outdated norm. And no, the authors of this book are not antimen, or ageist. It's just that there's such a wealth of experience that people could unlock and release to the benefit of themselves and others.

By presenting a monoculture, organizations are held back from tapping into the unappreciated talents and dormant skills. It's time to break the stereotype, and leave the hero leader where he belongs, on our TV and cinema screens. We're now entering a new era of leadership, where diverse and inclusive leadership brings individual and organizational benefits.

It's Time for the Era of Abundant Leadership

Let's be clear; this is not news. It's just that abundant leadership and better leadership behaviors are urgently needed in this "VUCA World" of volatility, uncertainty, complexity, and ambiguity.

Back in 1989, Professor Harold Schroder[1] told us that the hero leader myth had been debunked. Earlier researchers had already shown that "heroic leadership will decrease effectiveness of organisations."[2] Yet the myths persist. And behaviors need to change. The authors covered some of the arguments for change in our contribution to the book *Breaking the Zero-Sum Game*,[3] listing the very real performance and financial benefits to organizations of more inclusive and diverse leadership. The time is long overdue for transformation—away from solitary hero leaders to a more abundant, inclusive world of leadership. But this new world of leadership needs support and encouragement. It's time for those responsible for their own, and others', leadership development to empower abundant leadership. *It's time to celebrate the emergence of abundant leadership.*

Abundant leadership is where men and women, young and old, of every culture, step into leadership roles (not positions) regardless of their status, power, or society's expectations. The gender-linked benefits for the United Kingdom[4] alone are estimated at £14 billion, which doesn't include the benefits of culturally diverse or age-diverse leadership.

We want to support the emergence of abundant leadership, and our approach comes from asking two fundamental questions:

Q. What's needed and what works?
A. *Transformational Leadership Works*

You don't need the latest fad—the flavor of the month. What's needed is an intelligent, systems-wide application of consistent, high-performance, emotionally intelligent behaviors that flex to the context and changing situations faced by managers daily. And, to quote a 2012 study[5] "transformational leadership is most strongly associated with the implementation of diversity practices."

There are visible, measurable behaviors: leadership styles that really inspire and motivate people, underpinned by the less visible everyday conversations managers have and their invisible attitudes and values. This combination makes a positive difference to team members and a positive contribution to organization success.

Today's leadership development programs seem to focus on delivering today's tactical solutions. That's fine, as far as it goes. You need leadership that's going to take your organization from where you are today to where you need to be tomorrow—and the day after—because the world is changing rapidly and the solution is transformation.

Q. How do you achieve transformational leadership?
A. *Include people focused methods that result in transformational outcomes*

Organizations say they need transformation; yet employ transactional techniques. Because when they see what's involved, they back off.
There are two reasons why this happens:

> If you want to go fast, go alone. If you want to go far, go together.
> —African Proverb

If your job is in the "change" or "transformation" department, you'll appreciate this rationale quickly. You'll also likely have the tools to understand and implement change. Organizations want to see change happen quickly. And the bigger challenge is to bring people along in that transformation: to go far and go together. What this means, in practice, is the Change team working closely with the HR and Learning and Development (L&D) teams, creating an environment where abundant leadership is valued, and where individuals can develop new skills and feel safe to apply them back in the workplace. Another quote:

> If you make people think they're thinking, they'll love you. If you really make them think, they'll hate you.
> —Don Marquis

There's a real need to overcome the resistance to change and to help people feel safe to address the challenges of transformation. We use the word *safe* because that's what people tell us they need—a safe space to address challenges, to try out new ways of working, and to embed better management and leadership practices.

We see our purpose in writing this book as aligning the individual need to develop leadership skills, with the organizational need to provide the means to develop, and the environmental need for a culture in which that development can succeed. It's not one thing or another; it's all these elements. Then, people can be fulfilled and organizations can be more successful.

We don't see our job in writing this book as taking you through a step-by-step checklist of things to do. Rather it's a book to get you thinking, hopefully talking, and ultimately getting into action around individual and organizational leadership development needs. According to the United Kingdom's Chartered Management Institute, only one in five managers have a recognized management qualification.[6] And developing an abundance of leadership is at the heart of transformation. Clearly, if we're going to upskill leaders and managers, we all need to know what works. And knowing what works creates an abundance of leadership and a reduced reliance on individual hero figures.

We need the courage to transform: transform our own leadership, support, and empower others. We need the determination to enable a higher performing leadership culture in our organizations. Courage is usually seen as the epitome of the hero leader. But we're asking you not to be a lone hero. We're asking you to find allies so that you make change, and move forward, together. So here's the deal-breaker question: ***Are you ready for the leadership gamechanger?*** This isn't just about you as an individual leader; it's also about organizational culture having the collective courage to achieve transformational leadership. So often managers leave leadership training courses nurtured with lofty ideals and leadership aspirations, only to return to a nest of vipers.

One of our students told us this story:

> I used to help my Dad clean out the fish tank. He'd carefully take
> out each of his precious fish collection, quickly dipping them in

a small clear water tank. With my help, he'd rigorously clean out the display tank and gently return the fish. We'd literally see them in a new light: the iridescent colors of the little neon fish were my favorites.

Why would you invest in training up leaders only to return them to the dirty water? Especially when what you thought was a fish tank turns out to be a shark tank. What's needed is a whole-system approach to better leadership, and this book helps you consider the whole "heroic system," rather than focusing solely on individuals, such that when we've invested time, effort, and money in their development, the environment they return to is ready for them too.

Forton Leadership and Coaching: Our Story

After 25 years in corporate life as leaders ourselves and fifteen years developing others, we paused to take stock of what worked. What do we notice about the most successful leaders? What lessons have we learned? What did we learn from our own students? And indeed, from our own failures! Some factors are irrelevant. Leadership can emerge anywhere—wherever someone is ready, willing, and able to step up and take responsibility.

We see our role in leadership development as drawing the route map to better leadership—setting out the skills, behaviors, and character traits that support more successful leadership. We've taken that experience and distilled it into our leadership model. We've taken it into our coaching business too.

Bob Hughes created the Professional Leadership Coach Training Programme, the first of its kind to be accredited by the International Coach Federation back in 2002, and it was Helen who managed that process. Then we acquired the *My360plus* leadership psychometric based on the Schroder high-performance behaviors model so that we can support people, step by step, to appreciate their strengths, neutralize their weaknesses, and value the contribution of others in the abundant leadership mix. Today, we work with leaders and managers around the world. We feel proud to work across culture, age, and gender. We see our role as encouraging people to bring out the best in themselves and others, not to impose a single method or approach on people.

It may sound paradoxical to talk about making transformational change "step by step," starting from where you are. We're more used to the heroic figure making sweeping gestures and pointing toward the glorious future. Yes, we strongly believe in having a clear vision, and we also know that real change making relies on systematically and consistently putting one foot in front of another. We value the day in, day out, spadework as being as much value as the inspirational oratory, complete with stirring music and mood lighting. Maybe that's why we've been described as having the best leadership and coaching model out there. But don't take our word for it; jump over to our website and find out for yourself. (https://thefortongroup.com)

Coaching: The Game Changer in Transformational Leadership

Leadership coaching goes to the heart of how every leader and manager deals with his or her people and delivers for the organization.
Leadership coaching:

- Delivers meaningful ROI
- Personalizes and embeds learning
- Addressed any topic
- Catalyzes good ideas into reality and performance
- Deals with the complexity of organizational dynamics and culture
- Touches the heart of peoples' values and motivation

Now, let's be clear. When we say "leadership coaching," we mean support from coaches properly trained, accredited, and experienced in the skills of leadership and development. International qualifications matter to us. Our methods show equivalence of qualifications across educational boundaries and barriers under two banners, namely, the International Coach Federation (ICF) and the Chartered Management Institute (CMI), a UK-based standards body issuing professional qualification programs, so that, despite differing national frameworks, a leadership qualification in one country is just as relevant to leaders in another. We also support the development of leaders' and managers' own coaching skills so that supportive performance and motivational conversations become routinely and easily used. We call this "everyday feedback," where reviewing what works is a developmental routine between peers, not a remedial dressing down from the boss.

Transformational Leadership: A Defined Skillset

Leadership and management is vital to organizational success. And it's a skillset; yet despite the global market in MBAs, the topic of "leadership" itself, and the skills that support better leadership, are not embedded in MBA curricula. Some might argue that it doesn't need to be limited solely to business management—that it's a core skill set for all organizations, at all levels.

The Chartered Management Institute,[7] in its February 2018 report, gave its number one recommendation for "Developing 21st-Century Leaders" as "Give all learners management and leadership skills to improve employability. Opportunities to develop management, enterprise and leadership skills should be made accessible to students in any discipline, as well as those on business and management courses."

Using the Forton leadership model, professionals responsible for developing and coaching leaders have a simple, yet transformational, way to support leadership success in any part of the organization. And leaders and managers can invest their time and effort in working toward meaningful qualifications that cross organizational and cultural boundaries. It means a focus on what works in leadership development, based on managers' and leaders' real-world experience, as well as peer-reviewed academic research. This means that, from the first 360 exploration of leaders' behaviors, through to one-to-one coaching and peer action learning, employers can be confident that a qualified manager has the knowledge and skills to be a successful leader for that most precious of resources—their people.

Thanks to word of mouth through our clients, we reach across the world through our partners and through a network of experienced trainers, consultants, and coaches. The old barriers to better leadership need no longer exist, thanks to today's cutting-edge technology. Everyone can benefit through e-learning, online live learning, coaching by VOIP, or in-person development. This means we can reach leaders on every continent, wherever they are, without imposing our culture on others. And we can touch their lives and the lives of people who work with them. Most importantly, it means we can drop the many myths of leadership and distinguish between leadership fact and fairy story. So that's enough about us. What about you?

Your Story: Why Read This Book

This is a book for taking leadership development into your own hands and for influencing the organization around you to be better prepared for the abundant leadership revolution. This book is for you if you need to develop your own leadership skills to:

- Be a better, more confident leader
- Be a more engaging, coach-like leader
- Define the kind of leadership your team needs
- Identify the skills core to your success

And it's for you if you're responsible for developing leadership capabilities in your organization to:

- Uncover the untapped talent in your organization and give people the best chance of success
- Explore whether to develop from within or bring talented people in from outside
- Be careful about costs and invest in people development

It's for you if you want to transform this know-how into sustained and successful delivery back in the workplace. And if you're not asking any of those questions, maybe you're just interested in how best to grow leadership as a theoretical exercise and want to hear about our approach. This book is for people serious about growing themselves, their team, and their organization, committed to delivering real change and transformation, and making a real difference to their own lives and the communities around them.

Why Challenge the Hero Myth?

The hero is the defining myth of leadership development: the need for a "hero" and how that person looks and behaves. The hero myth underpins current approaches to leadership. Multimillion budgets are committed to keeping it going. It's currently the dominant leadership development paradigm.

In this book, we explore, question, and challenge these hero notions. For example, the myths that:

- Organizations need a hierarchy with a hero at the top
- Any one person has all the answers
- Gender, culture, or the color of someone's skill makes a difference to his or her leadership potential

We're not antihero—far from it. We're delighted that there are more and more diverse role models for leadership. But we take time to be clear about what a real "hero" is—separating the fantasy from the facts.

How This Book Is Structured

We've divided the book into four key sections, based on the FortonD^4 leadership development model, created by the Forton Group. And we've provided a separate stimulus questions for you at the end of each chapter. So that you can reflect on, and deliver, the kind of leadership you need.

The FortonD^4 Leadership Development Model

- Define your leadership needs
- Discover and retain the talent(s) you already have
- Develop people and create a learning environment
- Deploy: support leaders to apply their skills

The beauty of the D^4 method (Figure 1) is that it's a systematic approach to thinking through this process, for optimum success. It works both at the individual and at the organizational levels. It works for people developing others and for those developing themselves.

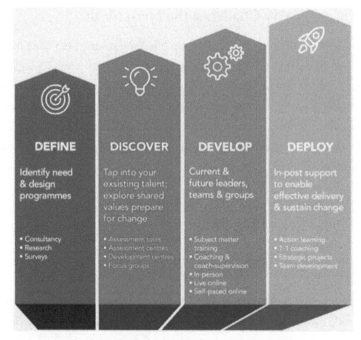

Figure 1 The FortonD^4 leadership development model

Source: © The Forton Group Ltd., 2018.

D^1: DEFINE. Tailor Leadership to Your Needs

At a client meeting, we asked what success would look like. What was important about developing the leadership capabilities of the organization? This stopped our client in his tracks, because it hadn't been defined. And yet the organization was willing to invest significantly in its leadership development program.

Your organization, department, or team is unique. Identifying the right leadership mix is vital to success. Part 1 looks at the issues you may want to consider.

Leadership Development: A Solution Looking for a Problem?

In Chapter 1, we look at the solo leader hero myth and the need for more balanced, more inclusive, leadership. We explore barriers to developing a high-performing leadership culture. In this zone of discovery, we encourage questions about what kind of leadership the organization needs to be successful and where to start—because that may not be leadership development. Better teamwork or improved employee engagement may be higher priorities.

Leadership: Problems or Puzzles?

In Chapter 2, we explore different ways of defining the leadership development challenge: as a puzzle or a problem. We focus on the new paradigm of leadership development to meet the challenges of "VUCA World." VUCA World is the place created by the volatility, uncertainty, complexity, and ambiguity faced by leaders, which requires a different approach to dealing with the situations they face and a new approach to leader development.

No Cape Required

We all know it's a myth that one, cape-clad hero can save the day. But we still cling to it. It's time to throw off the cape, and the underpinning beliefs, assumptions, and unconscious bias tucked under it. Chapter 3 explores these dominant paradigms and the benefits, for organizations, teams, and individuals, of making change.

D^2: DISCOVER

The discovery phase offers new ways of looking at talent selection and contests the practice of recruiting for cultural "fit" when that may not be what's needed.

Brokering Peace in the War for Talent

In Chapter 4, we challenge the "war for talent" metaphor and argue instead for a more collaborative approach to recruitment and retention. We look at the benefits of in-house talent nurturing versus the costs (in time, not just in money) of hiring from outside.

Mining for Gold

"What's the definition of an expert? Someone from a different country."
(Anonymous)

In Chapter 5, we address the myth of shiny suited outsider, or the knight in shining armor, and invite you to dig a little deeper into your talent pool. It's easy enough to see why people fall for these myths; they're enticing and seem to solve our problems in a moment. We explore the allure of the hero myth, and the risks.

Filling the Vase

In Chapter 6, we explore approaches that value every member of the team for his or her diverse contributions, rather than the "zero-sum game" of winners and losers. We need to bring reward systems closer to real contribution, as these get "gamed" by people looking to beat the system.

D³: DEVELOP

For development activities to be worth their investment, they need to be skills based, change behaviors, and be genuinely useful in the work place. In this section, we explore some of the shifts in thinking about leadership development for leaders to succeed in VUCA World.

Soft Skills Are Tougher Than They Look

In Chapter 7, we challenge the labelling of empathy, compassion, and collaborative skills as "soft." In today's world of work, relationships and communications between people are vital. Developing these skills is at the heart of succeeding in VUCA World.

Leadership by Lion Taming

Part of the challenge of the hero myth is that leadership development programs support that myth; it's a symbiotic relationship that exists only to support the development of heroic leaders. Chapter 8 goes more deeply into the specifics of leadership behaviors and their adaptability.

Nobody's Perfect

Having talked about virtue though, it's time, in Chapter 9, to look at the shadow side. Leadership is a daily practice—a journey, not a destination. That means we practice, and sometimes fail, to be a good leader. Nobody's perfect, yet hero figures are expected to succeed, or risk being seen as "failures." It's vital that we address attitudes toward failure and the fear of failure.

D^4: DEPLOY

It's not enough to invest in peoples' development then throw them, unsupported, back into an unchanged work environment afterwards. New skills and behaviors need time to bed in. We argue for deployment support programs, including one-to-one and group coaching, mentoring, and PALS (facilitated Peer Action Learning Sets) that support and actively encourage people to deploy their new skills. Optimum deployment is also about the wider environment and introducing new ways to develop more abundant leadership.

Leaders: A Higher Life Form?

In Chapter 10, we support the view that the leadership skillset needs to be introduced and developed in people as early in their career as possible. We explore the notion of leaders as "better than," in some indefinable way, than managers or team members, when what we need in today's world of work are resourceful enablers who motivate and inspire each other, and—working together—get the job done.

Are Interviews Just Rose-Tinted Views?

In Chapter 11, we question whether interviews are just an expensive method for looking at people through rose-tinted spectacles. It's time to acknowledge how we're seduced by beauty parades and get past our unconscious biases, so that we truly get the best people for the role.

Wanted: Sharp People and Well-Rounded Teams

Chapter 12 explores the notion of "well-rounded people" and the desire to iron out their wrinkles, rather than accept sharp—and even flawed—individuals who, working together, are willing to make up a well-rounded team.

What This Book Doesn't Cover

- Performance-Related Pay
- The gender–pay gap
- Whether leaders are born or made

These myths have been extensively addressed elsewhere.

The "No Cape Required" Worksheets

This book comes with stimulus questions at the end of each chapter to get you started. They are deliberately incomplete—your challenge is to discover the questions you should be asking about leadership in your organization, and in your own life.

We've been deliberately provocative and deliberately vague. No two organizations are alike, however much we may compare ourselves to others. So, as well as personalizing your own learning and development, we encourage you to personalize the process that gets you to the best possible L&D for your organization.

These starter questions are there to stimulate your thoughts and discussions.

Now you've got the overall picture, let's drop those capes and dive in . . .

Notes

1. H.M. Schroder. 1989. *Managerial Competence* (Iowa, IL: Kendall Hunt).
2. D.L. Bradford and A.R. Cohen. 1984. *Managing for Excellence: The Guide to Developing High Performance in Contemporary Organizations* (Hoboken, NJ: Wiley), quoted p.32, Managerial Competence, (ibid).

3. R.N. Hughes, and H.R. Caton-Hughes. 2017. Ch.14 "The Inclusive Leader at the Centre of an Interconnected World." In *Breaking the Zero-Sum Game: Transforming Societies through Inclusive Leadership*, ed. A. Boitano, R. Lagomarsino, and H.E. Schockman. Bingley, UK: Emerald Publishing.

4. F. Lagerberg. 2015. "The Value of Diversity (Report)," Grant Thornton, http://www.grantthornton.global/en/insights/articles/diverse-boards-in-india-uk-and-us-outperform-male-only-peers-by-us$655bn, (accessed May 2, 2016).

5. E.S. Ng and G.J. Sears. June 2012. "CEO Leadership Styles and the Implementation of Organizational Diversity Practices: Moderating Effects of Social Values and Age." *Journal of Business Ethics* 105, no. 1, pp. 41–52.

6. Chartered Management Institute. June 2017. *Leadership for Change: CMI's Management Manifesto* (London, UK: Chartered Management Institute), p. 6.

7. Chartered Management Institute. February 2018. *21st Century Leaders: Building Employability through Higher Education* (London, UK: Chartered Management Institute).

CHAPTER 1

Leadership: A Solution Looking for a Problem?

People who enjoy meetings should not be in charge of anything.
—Thomas Sowell

It's time to explore the myth of hero leadership and why we believe that inclusive, abundant leadership is the better option for the 21st century. At the same time, this means looking at the challenges for leadership development and prioritizing that investment. At an individual level, it means flexing between a range of core leadership behaviors and styles, depending on the needs of the team, department, or division, not just the overarching needs of the organization. This is a vital first step. No leadership development activities should take place without clear definitions of an organization's purpose and leadership needs.

Development and Reward Mechanisms

Sitting in a presentation, the new owners painted the picture: we were on the cusp of greatness, on track to be one of the top five UK financial institutions. Its growth—in the dawn of the digital era—was to be delivered by collaborative cross-selling between operational centers that offered different products. We were taken on a boat trip on London's River Thames to celebrate the takeover. We were shown an "inspirational" video.

To embed this new dawn, and introduce our leaders to new ways of working, the top team were transported to the beautiful English Lake District for an energetic program of development activities. Our MD became the oldest man to abseil down a forty-meter crag. The top team sang campfire songs in the bus on the way back to London and greeted one another heartily in the office corridors.

And yet what changed? Within weeks, old ways of working were back. And worse, an "us and them" mentality grew up among the very people who were meant to be collaborating, as competitive internal behaviors created win/lose mentalities. And the digital revolution was won by organizations with the biggest purses. The new owners retreated, licked their wounds, and lived to fight another day.

It's not a tale of disaster. At that time, the City of London was one of the world's largest financial centers. Regardless of political change, it has an essential strength in its position. Get in early and you can trade with Japan and the Far East; come the afternoon, North America wakes up and there's a big business to be done.

That organization is now truly global, with a significant European headquarters building dominating the city skyline. The time just wasn't right for its ambitions. However, we would also argue that the City of London, like other financial centers, has suffered from the core myth of leadership: competition to reach the pinnacle of a solo leader.

Macho males demand ever higher risk-taking. Charismatic leaders pull the wool over the eyes of those people in place to ensure governance. Boardroom battles led to eye-watering salaries and bonuses. Investment in IT systems did not deliver. Mergers and acquisitions made no sense.

This win/lose mentality stems from development investment and activities that promote the hero leader myth. The point of this story isn't to take a pop at any particular leadership development program. It's to pose the following questions: Is leadership development the solution? Or is it actually part of the problem? What problems is it solving or creating? And what kind of leadership is truly needed for this, specific, organization? Setbacks are common in organizational development and don't equate to "failure"—yet how can we reduce organization development risks and improve success rates?

Good leadership plays an important part in today's rapidly changing world. Change itself, the complexities and uncertainties, and the volatility and ambiguities faced by people every day mean that it's a must. But more of the same is not the right answer. Any organization that perpetuates traditional stereotypes and puts a man at the pinnacle of the organization, hero-like, with his cape flapping in the wind, is not going to be the most successful.

It may be "successful enough" for some, but as shareholders discover the hidden price paid for the 19th-century practices in the 21st-century climate, why settle for the second best when there's so much untapped talent?

This isn't an "anti-man" diatribe either. The gender of the person at the top isn't the issue. Women are as likely to believe the hero leader myth and fall into its trap as men. And the media loves the "fallen hero" myth. It builds up people and tricks them into believing that they really are that hero. It keeps audience figures up with each new twist and turn in the plot. And when leaders fail (as inevitably they do), the media are baying for blood. And the organization sees the solution as simply replacing the old hero with a new one.

Yet where's the evidence for an "abundant leadership" model?

A 2011 UK Parliament report quoted a European research that showed that "strong stock market growth among European companies is most likely to occur where there is a higher proportion of women in senior management teams[1]" and that companies with more women on their boards were found to outperform their rivals with a 42% higher return in sales, 66% higher return on invested capital and 53% higher return on equity.[2]

A 2015 Grant Thornton report[3] showed that companies with diverse executive boards outperform peers run by all-male boards, based on listed companies in India, the United Kingdom, and the United States. This is not news. As a 1994 U.S. report[4] put it: "diversity in the workplace is profitable."

Organizations which excel at leveraging diversity . . . will experience better financial performance in the long run than organizations which are not effective in managing diversity.

Note the words "proportion" and "diversity" by the way. What we're talking about here is what we call "balanced boards." And if you're a limited company, why wouldn't you want to tap into a 42 percent higher return on sales? If you're a shareholder in that company, why wouldn't you want to see a 66 percent higher return on invested capital? Or a 53 percent higher return on equity? All of this without any increase in costs. The belief that the solution is power in the hands of a single person is what gets in the way of success. When staff and shareholders see that the only thing standing in their way to greater success is a collective myth of the hero leader; and that all that's needed to get started is a shift toward a more inclusive, more abundant, leadership, then the game is afoot.

A different approach to leadership, tailored to the needs of the organization, is needed. Leadership is delivered by the abundance of talented people across the organization, who each contribute their different skills, strengths, and experience to a cohesive whole. This book is not about targets for diversity and inclusion, or new legislation. Our focus is the development of abundant leadership so that organizations have the capabilities to better succeed. The Forton Group's Abundant Leadership Model, where emotionally engaging styles (based on the Goleman et al.[5] model), observable behaviors (based on the Schroder[6] high performance model), within an ever-changing context, is central to this book (Figure 1.1):

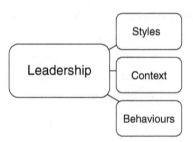

Figure 1.1 The Abundant Leadership Model; develop leadership behaviors and engaging styles, appropriate to the context

Source: © The Forton Group, 2018.

We're using words like "abundant," "inclusive," and "engaging" to describe this next level of leadership development. However, we encourage you not to get hung up on the adjectives, because it's about the kind of leadership your organization needs, not our definitions. We're using "abundant" because we like it best. You get to choose the word you prefer.

Once the organization has addressed the central questions about what it needs to be successful in the future, a picture of the needed balanced leadership profile will emerge. And if people see that more women, younger people, people from diverse backgrounds, experience, and talents are needed, then they can be supported and developed to achieve those goals.

The "Hero" Is Dead: Long Live True Heroes

Since we're no longer talking about "hero leadership," let's regain the lost meaning of the word "hero" and confine it to the people in our society who truly deserve the term—the "Gold Star" heroes; the work of our blue light services; the lifesaving successes of our doctors and nurses; or people fundraising for their favorite charity, whose crazy challenges really do translate into scientific breakthroughs.

The myth of the hero leader is embedded in our cultures. As Joseph Campbell's scholarship[7] into archetypal mythologies demonstrated, the traditional hero leader who was called by need to slay the dragon, rescue the princess, and return home with treasures is global. The need to be a hero in the eyes of others is a primal one—to demonstrate strength, cunning, and, ultimately, wisdom. Of course, many heroes fail at that last hurdle.

Yet just as we no longer send men out to hunt for woolly mammoth or saber-toothed tigers, we no longer need that stereotype at the pinnacle of organizational power. It's a tough myth to bust. Hero films, featuring ever more battles between "superheroes," are being made at an increasing rate since 2000 and have never been more popular. There's a problem with this: the target audience[8] for these films are young males, aged 12 to 18 years, with older men as the secondary audience, reliving their comic-reading youth.

The dragon we need to slay today is the hero myth that's stuck in the past, in a nostalgic memory of male youth. One part of the myth that everyone prefers to forget is the annual replacement of the hero. An individual was given elevated status, but only for a defined period of time, before he was slain and replaced. Another part of this myth is about going solo. Don't people watch what happens when someone says, "let's split up" in those superhero films?

So, let's slay these "solo hero" myths and get real about developing leadership. It's not that we're killjoys, out to spoil peoples' fun or dismiss popular culture. We're far from it. The point is that it's great in the movie world but dysfunctional in the world of organizational development. Today's world of work demands different realities, not yesterday's myths.

Hero leadership masks other problems, too. It's closely allied to the "command and control" myth, where that leader believes that success comes from telling people what to do and "what's measured, gets done." This functional, transactional approach to leadership and delivery just isn't enough anymore. It's fine if we're talking about widgets or any kind of product that needs a consistent quality, churned out day after day. And even there, a more inclusive style of leadership will be more successful.

Going back to our aging leaders abseiling down the cliff front, the mythical and heroic style of physical challenge, embedded in the dark ages, really didn't address that organization's needs. Saluting someone for that achievement perpetuates the single hero leader myth, when the organization needed better collaboration and communications. They needed to get over their competitive mind set, not embed it.

These are specific leadership behaviors that can be developed in people willing to make that mindset shift. And it makes sense to identify people who have innate talent in this, as a starting point. Their age, gender, or culture are no bars to these ways of working. Once we've separated the real needs and contexts from the outdated myth of hero leadership; when we identify the needed leadership behaviors and styles, we can finally get to grips with the issues.

Today's Abundant Leadership Is about People Who Care

As part of a talent management program, I worked with a leader running a factory making the cement for joint operations (hips and knees, typically). What was once a rare and risky intervention to reduce pain and restore function is now routine; these operations transform peoples' lives.

As well as the skill of the surgeon and operating team, there are two key elements that need to be at a consistent high quality: the replacement joint and the cement that fixes it in place. As you'd expect, the cement is made in strict and clinically clean conditions to a tight specification. Even small variations in the environment can render batches unusable—at great expense. The organizational challenge is to get it right, every day.

Telling wasn't the answer: people knew what to do. Nor was measuring, because a batch delivered is a batch completed, right? What's vital are the smallest details: changes in humidity; accuracy in the mix; ambient temperature. These are the tiny elements that made up the bigger picture. You need employees who are alert and responsive to the slightest variations. And the solution lay in looking at the employee-engagement scores. Compare the high-quality production shifts to that of the lower quality. Their levels of engagement, interest, and feelings of fulfillment in a job well done were noticeably different in both groups.

This is an example of abundant leadership: people leading from wherever they are, making the needed adjustments because they care about the details and the quality. Today, the power to make a difference lies at the edges, not at the center of command. The boss can't be there 24/7; collectively, the shift workers can. All of them can deliver technically; the challenge is to get them to care about the detail. No one should wait for someone higher up the authority chain to tell them to make adjustments, when the information that drives the decision is in front of them.

Valuing and applying employee-engagement methods are a success story that combines metrics with human behavior. It also demands a different style of leadership—people who can inspire, motivate, and support teams of people to work together and succeed, and to be genuinely interested in those tiny details that make all the difference. The good news was that this leader saw the need for a flex to a different leadership style and was willing to give it a go. And because the technical team was as willing as he was to achieve a more consistently high-quality product, they were open to a team response that led to reduced wastage and a more successful plant.

We're regularly asked to measure the impacts of our leadership development work or to produce evidence for employee engagement, both of which are achievable and affordable. Fewer organizations are willing to explore the impacts of poor leadership: the avoidable costs of wastage, yet this is where better leadership can have an impact. The most successful leadership programs start with this fundamental question: What kind of leadership does this organization need?

What Do We Mean by Leadership Development?

One size does not fit all. A sales or marketing function and culture will need a very different style of leadership to a technical, IT, or finance function and culture. At an individual level, organizations need to support leaders to develop their organizational awareness and decision-making skills so that their approaches are relevant to the context and make sense to people.

Help people understand that leadership **styles** are flexible. Different situations will demand different responses; from different people. Drawing on organizational diversity is a strength. Step one in the journey toward successful leadership development has to be identifying what you really need. And if the answer is better team work—from the top to the bottom in the organization—then traditional leadership development may get in your way.

Or it may be that tapping into your talent is the key first step. Look at people with potential who don't fit in the traditional mold of "leader." That includes women, young people, and those from different cultures to the majority, to escape from the leadership monoculture.

Understand the context within which you are operating, and can foresee operating, at your desired future point. Define the organizational purpose; align and adapt that for each part of the organization. For each part of the organization to be successful, look at the leadership behaviors needed for that part.

Leadership Development: Not the First Step

Leadership development is an integral part of the organizational improvement pipeline, but it's not the first step. To build capabilities, there are some questions to address along the way:

- Decide what kinds of leadership the organization really needs to be successful.
- Replace the competitive, solo hero mentality with balanced teams who work well together.
- Create a consistent leadership culture from top to bottom in the organization based on behaviors, styles, and context.

The question of purpose is vital: finding out what's important about achieving that vision as well as seeing and defining the vision.

It's important to make the purpose as tangible as possible: to identify what it's going to take to make this a reality and not let it remain a dream. You may need pioneers and iconoclasts to challenge the status quo. Or you may need your current leaders to develop their coaching and mentoring skills to support the emerging generation of leaders. Whatever you discover, we confidently predict that the answer won't be a rerun of the "hero leader" stereotype. It will be a more inclusive and balanced solution.

We also predict that leadership development will focus on behaviors, competences, and styles. And the right solution might be to invest in team building or employee engagement first, because you'll flex to your context, not an "off the shelf" solution. Whatever the solution for your organization, start with the key question, "What's the leadership your organization needs to make real the purpose you want?" This creates focus for your future success.

What's interesting about this method is that consensus reduces kickback. When people are invited to consider what's best for the organization, it depersonalizes the challenge. It helps to see the need in a less personal light and to see oneself as part of the solution. Because the experiences that gave people those gray hairs over the years are valuable, their insight and experiences can support the next generation of leaders to speed up their development. Mentoring and coaching helps today's top team feel connected to the future, in ways that create a win/win/win for the new leaders, today's leaders and the organization.

Use the *No Cape Required* Worksheet to Get Started

Get started with the *No Cape Required* worksheet; then build your own questions through a co-creative process with others to find out what questions you need to be asking about your own organization's leadership. Some of the methods come from the thinking behind paradigm shifts. The questions are designed to get the brain to step out of its normal transactional flow.

In this way, you'll discover the iconoclasts and the pioneers in your organization, ready to look at leadership in new ways. You'll also find the cynics who don't see the point, because, after all, nothing changes, right? And then you'll find a majority of people who, when presented with good ideas and compelling evidence, are prepared to give it a go and come along with you on the journey.

In Chapter 2, we explore different ways of defining the leadership development challenge: a puzzle or a problem?

Worksheet: Stimulus Questions

Flexing between a range of core leadership behaviors and styles depends on the needs of the team, department, or division, not just the overarching needs of the organization.

No leadership **development** investment or activities should take place without first clearly defining the organization purpose and leadership needs.

We call this the leadership development purpose vision statement. Use these questions to create your statement:

1. Paradigm shift question: What's impossible to do today in your organization that, if it were possible today, would fundamentally change the organization?[9]
2. The voice of the customer: What are customers and other stakeholders telling you?
3. Leadership development purpose: Create a leadership development purpose statement based around these questions:
   - What does success look like?
   - How will people know it's successful?
   - What will they be saying about the new leadership culture?
   - What values will still be important at that time?
   - What needs to be different to achieve this?
4. Suppose you wake up tomorrow and a miracle has happened: leadership in this organization has happened, exactly the way you hoped. What changed to make this happen?
5. Leadership development purpose vision statement:
   - From the answers to the questions above, create a statement that clearly and concisely states your leadership development purpose.
   - Feel free to play about with it, test it on friends and colleagues, and then edit it a bit more.

Notes

1. McKinsey & Company. 2007. *Women Matter: Gender Diversity: A Corporate Performance Driver* (Report) (New York, NY: McKinsey & Company).

2. L. Joy, N.M. Carter, H.M. Wagener, and S. Narayanan. 2007. "The Bottom Line: Corporate Performance and Women's Representation on Boards," *Catalyst*.

3. F. Lagerberg. 2015. *The Value of Diversity* (Report) (Chicago, IL: Grant Thornton).

4. U.S. Glass Ceiling Commission. 1995. "Good for Business: Making Full Use of the Nation's Human Capital: A Fact-finding Report of the Federal Glass Ceiling Commission," Washington, DC: United States Government Printing Office. http://digitalcommons.ilr.cornell .edu/key_workplace/116

5. See D. Goleman, R. Boyatzis, and A. McKee. 2002. *The New Leaders: Transforming the Art of Leadership into the Science of Results* (London, UK: Little Brown). (AKA "Primal Leadership in the US")

6. H.M. Schroder. 1989. *Managerial Competence: The Key to Excellence* (Dubuque, IA: Kendall Hunt).

7. J. Campbell. [1949] 2008. *Hero with a Thousand Faces*, 3rd ed. (New York, NY: Pantheon Press).

8. Superhero Films. https://brianair.wordpress.com/gcse-film-studies/ superhero-films, (accessed May 15, 2018).

9. With acknowledgments to Joel A. Barker, 2001. "The New Business of Paradigms," Classic Edition.

CHAPTER 2

Leadership Development: A Puzzle or A Problem?

Leadership is the art of getting someone else to do something you want done because he wants to do it.

—Dwight Eisenhower

A puzzle typically has a single answer; a problem has many possible solutions. So, do we see leadership and leadership development as a puzzle or a problem? If we see leadership as a puzzle, we'll develop people who meet the needs of a single problem. We may think we're being diverse, saying things like "Look, this puzzle has some straight-edge pieces and some middle pieces. Maybe we'll even put some quirky pieces in there too, just to mix things up a bit."

However you mix it up, a puzzle is still a puzzle. It has a right and a wrong answer. The pieces fit in their "right" places. Or they don't. It's a paradigm based on a "right/wrong" view of the world—fine for jigsaw puzzles, less so for organizational development.

Today's leadership and its development need a different worldview because we're living in a different era. This chapter looks at the new paradigm of leadership development to meet the challenges of VUCA (volatility, uncertainty, complexity, and ambiguity) World.

Introducing VUCA World

Today's leadership needs are more complex. There's the need for speed of response and flexibility, to deal with volatility; good decision making, based on reliable evidence, to deal with uncertainty; agility, to deal with the ever-present change; and parallel thinking; to deal with ambiguity. And yet it's more than that.

The good news is that no single leader needs to have all these qualities in abundance. The challenge is for leaders to discover the strengths and talents in the people around them and catalyze and develop their collective ability to deal with VUCA World. As Eisenhower said, "Getting someone else to get what you want done *because they want to* do it." This isn't manipulation; it's using the diverse strengths and talents of everyone in the team. Because people derive pleasure and fulfillment from working to their strengths; they want to use them. And because, in today's world there's no "correct" way of doing something; we need to identify and apply different approaches. This is important because, as one of our clients put it, "Our organisation needs to develop a learning mentality faster than the speed of change in our business environment" (CEO, Global Engineering Firm).

Many organizations create a set of capabilities or competences around leadership that start from a presumption of a single style of leadership: the one-size-fits-all approach. Yet we know that VUCA World is multifaceted. One person, one leadership style, is no longer tenable. We all need to flex. If your organization holds up certain people as role models, often those at the senior level, and consciously or otherwise, your learning and development team will create a cadre of leaders who fit in that mold.

Developing stereotypes when a range of styles is needed is like trying to stay rigid in a strong wind, when flexibility is the better response. Situations are no longer predictable, and because leadership is context specific, the need to develop flexible leadership styles, to suit different situations, is vital.

Different parts of an organization may require different styles of leadership. The nature of the role being managed will vary depending on whether it is a group of salespeople or a group of analysts or a group of creative thinkers. People will respond differently and have different needs to motivate and inspire them. This demands different leadership styles in those departments, and at different times.

Then, when we look at the evolution of an organization, the leadership style needed will vary.

The Dangers of Reverting to the Norm

I worked in one organization that had a new leadership team take over in a crisis: a classic turnaround situation where tight control and clear direction was needed. Over a period of about 2 to 3 years, the leadership team was very successful; the organization was performing well but was now constrained by that command-and-control style. To the credit of the leadership team, they saw this and tried to make change happen.

However, they were so used to managing in a particular way that they found it hard to shift. When they removed some of the controls, the minute something went wrong, their immediate reaction was to assume they'd made a mistake. As well as having no culture for living with the reality of the occasional "failure," they had no flexibility to adapt when things weren't going well. So they reimposed the controls back to the "right/wrong" puzzle mindset. They made key mistakes in their assumptions.

First, they assumed that people in the organization would immediately be able to switch away from the conforming style to which they had adapted as a response to the command-and-control leadership style. That would take time; it needed training. People needed to try it for themselves—be allowed to make mistakes and be trusted to fix them, before it became a reality. One leader even issued a diktat that there would be "no more command and control." He missed the irony there.

The second mistake the team made was to assume that they themselves could easily switch styles from commanding, to a more *laissez-faire* approach. If we habitually use only one leadership style, we may find it harder to switch and flex. One approach may be to switch the leadership team out. Yes, leaders can adapt from their default style and shift to managing and leading a very different way. However, that takes time, training and experience, and in this case, none of that was in place.

Another approach is to support people, one to one, during the transition phase. Coaching and mentoring are the two obvious solutions, and more of this later. Another supportive approach in this phase is Peer Action Learning (PAL), initially supported by a team coach, shifting to self-managed peer learning, once the teething problems are ironed out.

The Needed Paradigm Shift

Regardless of the eventual solutions, the paradigm shift is still needed:

- A conscious shift, away from traditional leadership styles
- Attitudinal shifts, away from a focus on "the" leader toward developing others and oneself: toward a leadership culture
- For the consistent application of a combination of the following competencies: intellectual intelligence, emotional intelligence, and managerial intelligence (IQ, EQ, and MQ)

For this paradigm shift to be enduring and inclusive, today's leadership needs to shift its focus—to "pan out" from a narrow focus on performance, from solely what it achieves, to a bigger notion of purpose. A sense of purpose not only encompasses successful delivery but also includes the "why," or values-based performance, and the "who," or the individual values, character, and behavior of leaders and managers. This is character-based leadership that consciously models the ideal of success, which includes everyone's strengths and contributions, based on values and targeted toward success.

The Evidence Base for This Shift

Applied emotional intelligence, for individuals and groups, comes from the key scholarship of the following people:

- Howard Gardner,[1] who first set out the notion of multiple intelligences;
- Daniel Goleman,[2] who built on Gardner's work and researched the evidence for applied emotional intelligence (EQ) in leaders;
- Dulwicz and Higgs,[3] who show how organizations can be more effective when EQ competences are embedded in organizational cultures.

This scholarship has led to the development of emotionally resonant leadership styles, which in some contexts can replace traditional commanding and pacesetting styles. It has also led to the recognition that it is a combination of competences that create better leadership and higher-performing organizations: traditional IQ, MQ, and EQ.

Traditional leadership styles tend to focus on the leader setting his/her direction and energy typically "commanding" or "pacesetting" in the Goleman et al.[4] terminology. The challenge with the commanding style is that it relies on orders flowing in one direction (from top to bottom)—useful in planning; great in emergency situations. However, overuse results in a dependent workforce and a leader/deputy leader structure.

Team members—who in today's world expect their contribution to be made, listened to, and responded to—become frustrated in structures that don't take their expertise, education, and strengths into account. It makes no sense to develop frustrated and dependent teams.

The pacesetting style may have its merits in providing effort and energy to get new projects off the ground. The challenge here is that in a world heavily reliant on the expertise of knowledge workers—as distinct from "widget makers"—predictability is no longer a given. There is also the danger of burnout if this style is used extensively.

VUCA World: The Key Leadership Challenges

The key leadership challenges of the 21st-century workforce include volatility, uncertainty, complexity, and ambiguity (VUCA). Look around: we're experiencing VUCA World right now. The #MeToo, #NeverAgain, #BlackLivesMatter, #BBCtransparency (equal pay), and other campaigns are all examples of people at the edges, using whatever influence they have to make change.

Each of these volatile forces contributes to unpredictability, so leadership has to orientate itself around those factors and no longer assume that a predictable pace can be set when factors change so rapidly. The most expensive examples of trying to force out-of-date thinking through pacesetting leadership are in the world of IT projects.

The Impact of Using Out-of-Date Thinking in a VUCA World

In the United Kingdom, it's estimated that the government lost £10 billion on the National Health Service IT project alone.[5] In the United States,[6] it's estimated that the Department of Defense has lost over four times as much money to canceled projects as the $20 billion lost by NASA in research and development programs.

It's unlikely that these countries are alone in their experiences, and these occurred, in part, because people in positions of authority applied rigid planning methodologies to transformational technologies. By contrast, products such as "Skype," one of the world's most downloaded software, have been developed more organically, where the actual product and customer base emerge from the interests of its developers. In the case of Skype, 5 people—2 Swedes and 3 Estonians—were the founding team.

Methods such as "Agile" and "Scrum" have arisen in the place of a top–down, pacesetting leadership style, summed up by statements such as "Build projects around motivated individuals," "Give them the environment and support they need," and "Trust them to get the job done."[7] We're not saying "agile" is the only solution; what we are saying is that team needs are different in different programs and projects, and leadership approaches need to be different too.

Einstein said, "Make things as simple as possible, but no simpler." Leadership may be complex. There may not be a single solution. Teams may have to adapt different working methods to address their environment. And this requires leaders, managers, and supervisors to appreciate that they need a range of responses and ways of working with their team members.

The Leadership Routemap™: Styles Plus Behaviors

Having a portfolio of leadership styles to call upon addresses the need to be more flexible in a complex and unpredictable world. EQ competencies underpin these styles and can be measured at individual and group levels. The work of Harold Schroder[8] and his team at Princeton University provided a clear high-performance framework that describes, and can identify, high-performing management and leadership competencies.

Four clusters summarize the competences: thinking, involving, inspiring, and achieving, "based on factorial studies of competency ratings for a number of managers."[9]

However, Professor Schroder makes clear that excellence does not rely on an individual alone: "Excellence is optimizing the range of competency contributions in a workgroup." This combination of high-performing be-haviors and applied emotional intelligence supports team building, better performance, and interdepartmental collaboration. We know that these leadership attitudes and behaviors work to deliver better leadership. Yet what is practiced is often a result of what today's leaders experienced in their development—the role models they had around them and how they behaved.

This combination of leadership styles (Goleman et al. defined six styles) plus high-performance behaviors (Schroder et al. defined 11 styles needed in the VUCA World) can create a "where do I start?" feeling. The good news is that you've done your homework following Chapter 1 and you know where you want to get to.

A client recently had one of those light bulb moments when we ex-plained this methodology to them. They had good technical experts in their teams, but these people were still applying old approaches to gen-erating income and value from their products and services. What our discussion helped them identify was a particular cluster of behaviors consistently missing in their leaders. This meant that the leadership development program had a natural starting place while continuing to value the existing team skills and strengths. The other good news is that when researching this book and applying what we learned in the world of work, we created the Leadership Routemap™ to map out this journey.

The beauty of a route map, and of seeing leadership development as a journey, is that people don't need to fit into a mold. Rather, questions are asked of them like the following:

- What leadership skills and behaviors do you already have?
- What leadership needs does your team have or this organization need?
- What are your development needs as a result?

Because before we start on a leadership journey, we may know where we're going, now we need to know where our gaps are and who's coming with us.

The Definition Gap: Abundant Leadership

So far, we've been describing "leaders" as those people at the top end of organizations, typically in positions of power. There's also a definition gap in defining what we mean by "leadership." It's not necessarily about position or power.

- Abundant leadership is based on the success and development of the whole team.
- Team success supports organization success, which, in turn, contributes to a more successful society.
- It's about influence more than power.

Where positional power was predicated on the value of budgets controlled, the number of people reporting, or the number of departments or offices under the leader's control, today's leadership is about how well a leader enables others to be successful and unlock their potential.

The authors' vision is for a world of work that grows leadership and supports a new type of leader:

People who role model authentic leadership, which springs from their values, who have a sense of vision and purpose.

People who take ownership and responsibility; who engage others, who listen and share a spirit of innovation and enquiry.

People who lead; not because it's in their job title, because they take ownership, contribute and deliver more.

This new type of leadership is one that makes the world of work a more fulfilled and effective experience.

—The Forton Group Ltd

In this definition, what makes a role a leadership role is the assumption of responsibility—stepping forward and driving decisions and actions, and being accountable to the team and the wider organization for their successful application. Yet, this points to two key barriers in the dominant paradigm of the hero myth: individual ego and the perceived threat to it from others.

In studies, people are, in theory, open to others and welcome their intelligence, but when theory shifts to real situations—such as meeting people in real life—they prefer being with people less intelligent than themselves. For example:

> Six studies revealed that when evaluating psychologically distant targets, men showed greater attraction toward women who displayed more (vs. less) intelligence than themselves.
> In contrast, when targets were psychologically near, men showed less attraction toward women who outsmarted them.[10]

These studies focused on personal relationships, but in the close working proximity of many organizations, it's easy to see how these behaviors might create unconscious bias in selecting the type of people that a leader might surround themselves with.

The second barrier is fear—the perceived threat of stepping out of line; being made to look foolish; or doing things differently. If the status quo rewards fitting in, going with the majority, or improving what already exists, then paradigm shifts won't happen. Supporting people to take calculated risks needs to be a key element of leadership development—to look at situations with fresh eyes and do things differently, even to fail.

There are leadership models that separate "technical" leadership from "project" leadership, or "people" leadership from "general" leadership. So those who feel more comfortable developing their technical expertise and less comfortable leading teams of people can do so, safe in the knowledge that they have a defined career pathway. It's still part of the wider abundant leadership pool. However, for some people, technology leaves them no choice. To paraphrase Shakespeare, leadership is being thrust upon them.

A client runs a technology lab where new technology has introduced laser systems for patient devices—a huge investment in technology, saving future space costs as well as speeding up the service. However, one challenge it posed that no one foresaw: lab technicians aren't always comfortable dealing directly with end users of the devices they make. They choose lab work so they don't have to interact. These are often the kinds of technical people we need to take on a leadership development journey. Knowing their working preferences and creating a development route map for them will impact on the leadership development program you eventually deliver and support.

New Definitions of Leadership

Every team member should develop their leadership qualities and apply them to their role. This is abundance. It's a behavioral model of leadership: a skill set that can be developed by anyone who is willing to learn and apply the skills.

Leadership behaviors are based on a foundation of self-awareness, of willingness to shift attitudes and grow skills. While traditional organizations separate out their communications departments or their learning and development, in VUCA World, every manager or leader needs to develop high-level communication skills and be equipped to support team learning and development. High-quality communication skills are an essential piece of the manager's toolkit in a VUCA World. It's just one example of the skills people need to develop—at any stage in their career.

An inclusive leader is an engaging leader: willing to engage not just in performance and delivery (the "what"), but in systems improvements (the "how") and personal, and people, development (the "who") as well. To make abundant leadership achievable, we look at it in four ways:

1. Leaders as people in responsible positions
2. Team leaders distributing leadership
3. Individuals contributing to leadership
4. Leadership as engagement with society

People who have chosen technical leadership need to understand their governance responsibilities and demonstrate competence and trustworthiness. Using communication skills as an example, they need to communicate well to share their knowledge and embed it within the organization.

In the case of lab technicians, it's vital that they develop good people skills to inform and reassure people, particularly hospital technicians working with vulnerable patients, where remarkable stories about creative solutions to help reassure people are emerging.

Project management calls for a more distributive leadership approach: where technical experts within the project are invited to contribute their expertise and encouraged to step forward with solutions and new possibilities. However, this form of leadership still relies on the person at the top "distributing" or bestowing leadership on the team. It requires a high level of transparency and role definition—or at least a definition of what "distributive leadership" means within any given context.

"Choosing partnership over patriarchy" is how Peter Block[11] described it in his seminal work on "Stewardship." When the approach to leadership is turned upside and team members are invited to contribute from a position of their strengths, talents, and experience (as distinct from having leadership distributed down to them), a more enabling or inclusive model is achieved. This method requires an understanding of every team member's contribution and the expectation of visible leadership: that all team members will contribute, speak up, and speak out.

Many organizations are already showing greater leadership in society through their corporate social responsibility (CSR) activities. Offering coaching, mentoring, and educational support schemes are typical examples. Providing work experience, internships, and work shadowing are all ways to raise peoples' aspirations, to support people returning to work, or to change careers in midlife. Beyond this application of leadership in specific contexts, there are consistent and measurable ways to develop inclusive leadership.

Inclusive leader profiling draws on Harold Schroder's work on high-performance behaviors, on diverse qualities, experience, and strengths. Not relying on "expert leaders," inclusive leadership is also emotionally intelligent.[12] We can develop leaders who create better working environments through influence and relationships, not power.

In essence, leadership is a series of visible, measurable behaviors, driven by invisible impulses: internal conscious and subconscious thoughts, attitudes, and feelings, which can be accessed only through self-awareness, reflection, and insight. If we are to make inclusive, abundant leadership a reality, then both visible behaviors and invisible impulses need to be addressed and developed.

To paraphrase Einstein, the challenge is not to overcomplicate or oversimplify leadership development. The challenge is that the further from the central idea one goes, the more complicated things become. The risk is that inclusive leadership development becomes so overcomplicated and the definitions so refined that people use complexity as a reason to not take action.

The Key Leadership Development Question

The question in developmental terms is, What support does a person need to become a more inclusive, engaging leader? While we may live in a complex world, the solution to handling complexity is not always more complexity. Additionally, when we create an environment of inclusive leadership around us, we create more resources to tap into: more potential answers and possibilities, not just in the people around us, but in the wider range of internal and external, visible and invisible resources available to us as well.

Leadership behaviors can be developed. They are not the preserve of the older people, the well educated, or the wealthy. They can be made easily available through our digitally connected world. Thanks to the power of the Internet, we can hold live video conversations across the world, or tap into self-paced learning resources at a place and time most convenient to ourselves.

This approach (known as "blended learning") means that the cost of leadership development can fall dramatically, putting it within everyone's reach. But there's no one single solution to the "puzzle"; the VUCA World is a series of problems with many solutions.

Voltaire said that "perfect is the enemy of the good," and it sums up the paradigm of the "correct" answer to a puzzle, on one hand, and the "best viable solution," on the other. If there's a model for an inclusive leader, it's the combination of intellectual intelligence, emotional intelligence, and management intelligence. Someone willing to switch attitudes away from the 20th-century leadership behaviors to embrace inclusivity is

- Willing to explore their own attitudes and feelings
- Willing to appreciate others' value: their strengths, motivations, values, and contributions

The people you'll want to take with you on this development journey will demonstrate potential, not just a past track record. Their communication styles will orient toward listening rather than talking, and asking rather than telling. They will judge, and be judged, on observed high-performing behaviors rather than "flavor of the month" leadership fads. They will take employee engagement seriously and turn plans into actions to benefit team spirit and the bottom line.

You may not be wholly certain that everyone will complete this journey. And while some people may have natural strengths among this skill set, these are developable skills. Today's technologies mean that development activities are more affordable for organizations that recognize the need for a journey through the VUCA World.

This is not a proposal for a "one-size-fits-all" model of leadership. Rather, this is a proposal for a process of leadership development that starts with the organization's needs and assumes that many untapped resources already exist within it. Tapping into these resources requires four key steps:

1. Defining the leadership need—through consultation and research (covered in Chapter 1)
2. Discovering the existing talent—regardless of age, gender, or culture
3. Developing people to meet the need
4. Deploying people while supporting them to deliver on their leadership potential

We'll cover points 3 and 4 in later chapters.

This notion of abundant, inclusive, and engaging leadership is not just a rationale for bringing more women into the boardroom, opening up to a more culturally diverse leadership team, or supporting young people to develop their talent. It's not just about improved performance or better results. It's a rational step with an ethical and moral base.

It makes sense to deploy and develop the most talented people in the team, regardless of their culture, gender, or age.

Worksheet: Stimulus Questions

We introduce the puzzle and problem paradigms, focusing on the new paradigm of leadership development, to meet the challenges of the VUCA World. The key challenge is to understand what the VUCA World looks like in your context so that you can apply the best leadership development solutions. These questions focus on the "PESTLE" (political, economic, social, technological, legal, environmental) analysis tool (Figure 2.1).

V = Volatility	C = Change
What's volatile in your organization, in your world or around the corner?	What changes are here, or on the horizon, that people need to address?
Political volatility	P
Economic volatility	E
Social volatility	S
Technological volatility	T
Legal volatility	L
Environmental/situational/contextual volatility	E
U = Uncertainty	A = Ambiguity
What are you, or others in your organization uncertain about?	What issues do people need to act upon without having all the facts?
P	P
E	E
S	S
T	T
L	L
E	E

Figure 2.1 VUCA world stimulus questions

Source: The Forton Group.

Please note: This is not to create a checklist of topics to address in leadership development programs; it's to help you see the VUCA World you're living and working in. The leadership development challenge is to find ways to live comfortably and flexibly in a VUCA World as it is.

Once you've answered the individual questions, sum up what your VUCA World looks like in a couple of sentences. And if your reflections have identified cultural or leadership gaps, summarize those too.

Notes

1. For example, H. Gardner. 1983. *Frames of Mind: The Theory of Multiple Intelligences* (New York, NY: Basic Books).
2. D. Goleman. 1995. *Emotional Intelligence* (New York, NY: Bantam Books).
3. V. Dulewicz and M. Higgs. 2000. "Emotional Intelligence—A Review and Evaluation Study," *Journal of Managerial Psychology* 15, no. 4, pp. 341–72.
4. See D. Goleman, R. Boyatzis, and A. McKee. 2002. *The New Leaders: Transforming the Art of Leadership into the Science of Results* (London, UK: Little Brown). (AKA "Primal Leadership in the US"), where the six styles are: "Commanding, Pacesetting, Democratic, Coaching, Visionary and Affiliative."
5. R. Syal. 2013. "Abandoned NHS IT System has Cost £10bn So Far," https://www.theguardian.com/society/2013/sep/18/nhs-records-system-10bn, (accessed April 4, 2018).
6. E. Elert. 2012. "NASA has Spent $20 Billion on Canceled Projects [Infographic]," http://www.popsci.com/science/article/2012-09/infographic-nasas-canceled-projects, (accessed April 27, 2016).
7. K. Beck, M. Beedle, V. van Bennekum et al. 2001. "Principles of the 'Agile Manifesto.'" http://agilemanifesto.org, (accessed April 16, 2018).
8. H.M. Schroder. 1989. *Managerial Competence: The Key to Excellence* (Dubuque, IA: Kendall Hunt).
9. Ibid, p.78.
10. L.E. Park, A.F. Young, and P.W. Eastwick. November 2015. "(Psychological) Distance Makes the Heart Grow Fonder: Effects of Psychological Distance and Relative Intelligence on Men's Attraction to Women," *Personality & Social Psychology Bulletin* 41, no. 11, pp. 1459–1473. http://psp.sagepub.com/content/41/11/1459
11. P. Block. [1996] 2013. *Stewardship: Choosing Service Over Self Interest,* 2nd ed (San Francisco, CA: Berrett-Koehler).
12. D. Goleman. 1995. *Emotional Intelligence*, op.cit.

CHAPTER 3

No Cape Required

Leadership consists of nothing but taking responsibility for everything that goes wrong and giving your subordinates credit for everything that goes well.

—Dwight D. Eisenhower

I was delivering a talk on leadership and was asked what single action might have the biggest impact on improving leadership. "Surgically remove the egos from your leaders" was my immediate and flippant response. In hindsight, that would be my considered response too.

Many of the famous books on leadership written over the last 40 years focus on leaders who have single-handedly transformed organizations. They often contain words of wisdom, pithy quotes, and maxims from "the great men" that have inspired and transformed the people in the organizations. These great men, and they usually are men, have been parachuted in to save a failing organization. Indeed, they don't even need parachutes; they have their superhero capes. All this makes for great reading and appeals to those of us who want to single-handedly bring change and transformation. It gives us hope and inspiration that we too can make that difference.

Many of the leaders we coach have a genuine desire to create a workplace that is better, successful, and, at the same time, has humanity at its core. Inevitably, people who have the courage to step up and try to make that difference will have an ego that supports them in their endeavors.

At one level that is fine; the original definition of the ego was just about a sense of personal identity. If we have a strong sense of our identity and feel a calling toward leadership, then of course we want that identity and character to spread out across the organization.

The ego has got a bad name over the years, and we often now equate it with an excess of self-worth and self-importance, often stepping over the boundary from confidence into arrogance. And that is the danger that happens with some leaders.

In this chapter, we address four key paradigms that, when shifted, have the potential to open up organizational success through the better utilization of all the skills and resources available to it. We look at ways to speed up paradigm change, through personal development and organizational change, and particularly by addressing unconscious bias, which takes care of the ego problems too.

Professor Archie Brown tells some cautionary tales in his book *The Myth of the Strong Leader*,[1] focused on the world of political leaders. It's a fascinating book, spanning democracies and authoritarian regimes and exploring leadership in many contexts. The lessons to be learned and the parallels to the world of organizations are many and varied.

Brown explores the quality of "strength" and why it seems such a common property we want to ascribe to our leaders. There are many qualities that political leaders need above and beyond the ability to look strong, yet it's the one we focus on. This focus on strength is another of the problems with the paradigm of the hero leader. Another important assumption coming from this notion, which needs to be challenged, is that this is the only model of leadership that can be successful. The danger of that is aspiring leaders attempt to shift away from their natural leadership preferences, driven by their own beliefs and values, and try, unsuccessfully, to emulate the superhero model. This, and related paradigms, are stifling organizations and preventing a glorious diversity of leadership that has the capacity to support organizations to survive and thrive in the VUCA World.

The four most notably out-of-date paradigms are:

1. The "hero leader" paradigm
2. The "male over female leader" paradigm
3. The "monoculture over diversity in leadership" paradigm
4. The "older over younger leader" paradigm

Combined, this is an ***exclusive*** model, or paradigm, of leadership.

The Hero Leader

Older men, from the same background, keep leadership to themselves and even feel heroic for doing so. They may see themselves as virtuous: like Atlas, taking the burden of the whole world on his back, protecting others from needing to carry the same burden—an obvious display of "strength." Or it may be that they have been seduced by the attention, the power, the place in society that the role of a leader bestows. The exclusivity paradigm may not be intentional, but it's not in the best interests of individuals, organizations, or societies.

The evidence for shifting away from this paradigm has been around for a while. It was challenged in 2004, in the Elsevier[2] *Leadership Quarterly* journal, which noted inverse correlation between performance and CEO charisma. "Never believe your own PR" is a famous maxim in marketing circles, yet this seems to be what happens. And it has knock-on effects. The effectiveness of their behaviors or the example they give to future generations are not valid considerations, even though they may mentor others.

The hero leader paradigm creates (typically) men who command in ways most often linked to crisis and conflict. They believe in hierarchy, have people perform routine tasks, and reject input from inferiors. These behaviors exclude others and cut the organization off from up-to-date thinking and the potential for better solutions. These leaders rely on the power of their personality, and feel rewarded by the size of their pay packet.

It's easy to see how this ego- and power-driven mindset, focused in the hands of a single person, led to many of the major corporate scandals of the 20th century, with overextension being a primary cause. Let's be clear here. We're not advocating getting rid of heroes—those people who, through effort, sacrifice, and commitment to others, perform amazing deeds. We're talking about replacing the paradigm of the hero illusion. People think that, by virtue of their position, they somehow magnetically attract heroic traits.

The charismatic hero leader paradigm currently prevails, yet it has a cost. For companies, it creates lost opportunities in terms of return on assets, estimated at over $655 billion in 2014.[3] In 2004, a report evaluated the links between "CEO charisma, compensation, and performance"[4] and found that while there was no correlation between charisma and performance, there was a significant correlation between a CEO's perceived charisma and their compensation package. Having charismatic men at the head of organizations costs more, has no performance impact, and keeps other talented people out.

The paradigm needed in today's volatile, uncertain, complex, and ambiguous world of leadership is abundant, inclusive, and engaging leadership.

Encourage Leadership Development in Women

One way to fill the gap is to welcome more talented women leaders. In March 2015, the UK newspaper *The Guardian*[5] reported that there were more men called John at the top of FTSE 100 companies than the **total** number of women at the top. Twenty-three percent of boards included women, and yet the goal was to have 25 percent representation.

In the United States, the organization 20/20 Women on Boards[6] reported that in 2015, "17.9% of corporate directors were women" (82.1 percent men); in Europe, all male boards had fallen to 5.4 percent from 21 percent in 2011.[7] A 2011 UK Parliament report quoted a European research that showed that "strong stock market growth among European companies is most likely to occur where there is a higher proportion of women in senior management teams"[8] and that "companies with more women on their boards were found to outperform their rivals with a 42% higher return in sales, 66% higher return on invested capital and 53% higher return on equity."[9] Ways need to be found to develop younger people and find leadership opportunities for them.

Diverse gender board leadership organizations outperform their male-only board rivals. "In the US, S&P 500 companies with diverse boards outperformed rivals by 1.91%. In the UK FTSE 350 the gap was 0.53% and for the Indian CNX 200, 0.85%,"[10] estimated at $567 billion, $14 billion, and $74 billion, respectively.

Encourage Leadership Development for People from Diverse Cultures

More diversity in terms of cultural leadership can also fill the gap. The UK National Health Service, available to every UK citizen and one of the world's largest employers, has over 1.3 million staff.

Just as public service employees should reflect the diversity of the population, its leadership should reflect that variety too. It's good for public health: diverse commissioning ensures everyone's health needs are addressed. However, according to a 2014 report,[11] "The likelihood of white staff in London being senior or very senior managers is three times higher than it is for black and minority ethnic staff."

Following are the organizational benefits of diversity:

- The Grant Thornton report,[12] based on listed companies in India, the United Kingdom, and United States, showed that companies with diverse executive boards outperform peers run by all-male boards.
- "Diversity in the workplace is profitable."[13] "Organizations which excel at leveraging diversity . . . will experience better financial performance in the long run than organizations which are not effective in managing diversity."

Encourage Leadership Development in Younger People

There's also a generational gap between older people holding power affecting young peoples' career paths. In 2010, the average age of an FTSE 350 board director was 58. In 2013, it was reported that "the average age of directors (68), average board tenure (8.7 years), and mandatory retirement age (72 to 75) have all risen."[14] A 2018 report by the UK's Chartered Management Institute[15] (CMI) develops its "work ready" thinking about the needs of young people entering the workplace.

In the UK, employers have long challenged the education that young people receive before they join the workplace, and the CMI has now identified so-called soft skills and the development of leadership behaviors, as part of the solution.

As a response to tragedy, the #NeverAgain movement has risen to challenge U.S. gun control laws, led by students. At the time of writing, it has had commercial impacts (with companies from airlines banks and car hire companies removing partnership arrangements with the US NRA organization) and social impacts, with legislation being discussed at state and national level. Yet the dominant paradigm (i.e., older people) has challenged the right of these people to be validated, claiming their age as a barrier to their right to leadership. The students immediately impacted by the gun tragedy that led to the movement have also been portrayed as "victims" and therefore, by implication, are less able to be "objective" about this highly emotive subject.

Inter-generational leadership matters in the workplace because today's organizational structures reduce traditional career paths. Young people can't climb the career ladders that previous generations expected. They may not be expecting those traditional career routes, but the ladders may not even be available to them. People say that "millennials" (the generation born just before, or maturing in, the 2000s) want more from their job than just an income.

Their social values are more evident, as is an expectation of involvement or consultation. Today's younger people are certainly more socially networked than connected to institutions.[16] As career paths become flatter and competition gets tougher, more people opt out of the journey altogether, which is a waste of talent. The career paths young people take matters because of the opportunity costs lost to organizations, not only in the churn of recruiting talented people, but also in the lost leadership and development opportunities that refresh organizations. Developing and retaining leaders within organizations is a reliable and cost-effective route to better leadership.[17] Meeting younger peoples' development needs is an investment in the organization's strategic future.

Change at Individual and Collective Levels

The CMI report[18] cites five skills and behaviors that employers want from 21st-century first-time managers:

- "Taking responsibility (60%)
- People management skills (55%)
- (Being) Honest and ethical (55%)
- Problem solving and critical analysis (52%)
- Collaboration and team working (48%)"

Leadership development is not solely about the development of the individual; nor is it just about team development. It's not enough to expect educational institutions, or in-house leadership programs, to develop people in this way. The wider environment also needs to shift.

For these investments to be successful, paradigm shifts at the collective (departmental or organizational) levels need to happen too. For example:

- Increase young peoples' involvement by rewarding them for their contribution, not their longevity.
- Provide leadership opportunities that stretch them.
- Move away from hierarchical organizations to networked organizations.

This approach is based, first, on the work of Ken Wilber and his "Whole Systems" model.[19]

The willingness to change needs to come from individuals **and** the wider culture: individual understanding of the behavioral shifts needed and a corporate structure aligned with the leadership need (see Chapter 1). The paradigm shift is needed in four ways; two at an individual level and two at a collective level:

- **Individually:** Internally shifting attitudes toward the abundant, inclusive leadership paradigm. Then, for individuals to demonstrate a behavioral shift that reflects a shift of attitude; where leaders model inclusive, high-performance behaviors.
- **Collectively:** Shifting group attitudes away from business as usual and toward a willingness to practice diverse thinking; then to make structural shifts in the organization that demonstrate the willingness to transform the environment.

UK-based business leader John Timpson wrote about his idea of "Upside Down Management,"[20] putting the success of his own (family-run, UK) business down to one factor: "It's the people who serve our customers who run the business and everyone including me are just there to help."

In today's knowledge economy, it's a reality that power is held at every level in the organization. This can have both positive and negative impacts. Think of the disgruntled employee who serves their revenge cold through saboteur behavior. While risk-avoidance methods are one part of the solution, enabling people to feel valued, equipped, and resourceful also pays dividends.

If the shift at an internal, attitudinal level is to make the effort to remove the ego and reduce the feeling of threat from those who are different from ourselves, the individual external action or behavior is to develop others. Timpson wrote a book to his son[21] on how to get through the minefield of running a successful business, reflecting another trait of the abundant leader: investing time and effort into developing others. This may mean nominating people who are best for a project; surrounding older leaders with younger, better educated people; and showing that leaders who do develop others are recognized and rewarded for dropping their egos.

Developing others is a key behavior in the Schroder high-performing behaviors in a VUCA World. It includes the behavior of giving feedback to stimulate better performance, coaching people, and ensuring they have access to training and development. This, in turn, creates greater consistency and more sustained excellence.

Leader Rotation

Another approach is to rotate leadership roles. The British academic and author Professor Mary Beard OBE wrote[22] about how her own Cambridge faculty rotates its chair every 2 years. At Plan International, a child-centered community development organization, people are promoted from country to regional director but revert after 3 to 4 years. This approach distributes wider experience of leadership among the group. Again, it challenges the dominant paradigm and has implications for how people are rewarded for their contribution.

New Structures at the Collective Level

De-layering and moving away from a strongly hierarchical structure is a paradigm shift. It is attempted in some institutions, yet often rejected by the people it's intended to set free from hierarchies. Yet, networked organizations are common in entrepreneurial organizations.

Buzzwords like "Agile" and "Scrum" reflect a simple, 21st-century truth: a job is just a job. A job, or role, is a collection of movable tasks that can be distributed around the team and play to peoples' differing skills, strengths, and relevant experiences. This construct has a greater need for leadership behaviors. People with a strong sense of responsibility are ready to be accountable, underpinned by values. But this isn't "leadership" displayed by a single person. Which is why we use the term "abundant" leadership.

It's very different from the traditional heroic leadership model. And the good news is that no cape is required. Indeed, no uniform, stripes on the shoulder, or other symbols of status or authority are needed in this new paradigm. We have the opportunity to release ourselves from outdated paradigms by diversifying and expanding leadership: holding managers and leaders to account against measurable competences and behaviors.

Abundant and inclusive leadership is a collective action or a series of actions. In the Wilber model, a collective, internal shift will define new models that value the enabling role of individual leaders and that enable a sense of group pride.

Address Unconscious Bias

For individuals and the collective, there is a key barrier to accepting new paradigms, whatever they are. It's the internal conscious and unconscious biases. We've already mentioned the power of the ego, when it's left unsupervised. It leads to a focus on the "me," not the "we."

Unconscious biases are sometimes also blind spots. We don't know what we don't know. It takes someone from outside to point out the problem. I literally have a blind spot in my car. Because of my height and the location of the driver's side mirror, there's a point at which if a car is overtaking my car, at one point in their maneuver, I can't see them. I'm glad I know this.

When I plan to overtake a vehicle, I deliberately move my head to visually check that blind spot. It could be a lifesaver. The most typical blind spot in the diversity, inclusion, and belonging agenda is not acknowledging one's own, or the organization's, bias against a group, or groups—not seeing or being willing to see (perhaps because of ego) the impacts.

This might be in teamwork, recruitment, promotion, or project allocation processes. When we make assumptions about a person, our bias creeps in.

The impacts it can have on the excluded individuals or groups include people feeling alienation or excluded. If they feel less able to be "themselves" (belonging), it becomes an emotional strain trying to fit in at work. Performance at work and relationships—at work and at home—suffer.

In the workshops we run, we use practical methods to address our individual and collective biases—starting with self-awareness of our own biases, then experiencing what it feels like to make the effort to consciously shift toward more positive and inclusive behaviors, then to explore the quick wins and the strategic changes needed back in the collective world to ensure that the structural environment is ready to accept a positive change.

Our goal is for the participants to feel "FAB," to

- Fit in, and then feel
- Acceptance, to acknowledge our biases and bring in
- Belongingness, so that people feel they fit in—It's a virtuous circle.

This takes conscious effort, personally and collectively. We invite participants to share the small steps they can make immediately and to take away ideas to develop with colleagues back in the workplace. The assumptions we make, about ourselves or others, are one form of unconscious bias.

In the workplace, it shows up in the "Comps and Bens" departments (compensation and benefits), where rewards and recognition schemes are based on the assumptions made by these specialist teams. I'm not saying their decisions are right or wrong. The challenge is to shift away from a global assumption that what motivates one individual motivates everyone.

In team settings, what motivates an individual leader may not motivate his or her team members. Individual shifts in assumptions, attitudes, and behavior alone are not enough. Inclusive leadership as a paradigm shift needs concerted effort and attitudinal and behavior change at the collective levels too, across teams, departments, and organization-wide activities, such as recruitment.

- Professional firms such as Deloitte have trialed hiding the name of applicants' universities to reduce bias. They've developed an algorithm "to consider 'contextual' information alongside academic results."[23]

- The BBC[24] introduced "name blind" recruitment to reduce unconscious bias against minority ethnic applicants.

At the heart of these paradigm shifts are new ways of understanding what drives autonomy and intrinsic motivation. It's a myth that one cape-clad hero can save the day. It's time to throw off the cape—it's no longer required. It's also time to throw off the underpinning beliefs, assumptions, blind spots, and unconscious biases.

The good news is that inclusive, abundant leadership works for everyone in the system. It delivers more for organizations at boardroom level and adds value across the organization, without overloading any one part of the system.

Worksheet: Stimulus Questions

In this chapter we address four key paradigms that, when shifted, have the potential to open up organizational success through the better utilization of all the skills and resources available to it.

- The "hero leader" paradigm
- The "male over female leader" paradigm
- The "monoculture over diversity in leadership" paradigm
- The "older over younger leader" paradigm

We also look at the blind spots, unconscious biases, assumptions, and ego-driven structures that hold back more abundant, successful leadership. We make a distinction between what individuals can do and what needs to change in the structure of the organization. If you recognize these traits, ask yourself (and others) the relevant questions below. Decide first whether you're asking these questions of yourself or an individual or as a team, department, or organization (collective):

Assumptions

- Personal Assumptions: What assumptions am I making about any given situation?
- Collective Assumptions: What assumptions do we make?

Bias Awareness

- When you catch yourself saying "should/shouldn't" or "must/mustn't," write it down. Learn to notice your bias and raise your awareness.
- Accepting and forgiving our own biases makes it easier to accept and forgive others.

Blind Spots

- Ask a colleague outside your team what "blind spots" they notice in your team. "What aren't we seeing?"
- The same for your organization: ask customers or others who know (and care about) what you do, what it is that the organization doesn't see, recognize, or value about itself?
- And what does the team/department/organization allow to continue that isn't good for its reputation, business, or development?

Structural Change

Assuming wider inclusion of abundant leadership from younger people, women, people of diverse cultures, or older people is possible, and there are no financial barriers or other resource constraints:

- What structural change would bring this about?
- What's the easiest change to make (quick win)?
- What's a change that's going to need collective, sustained support?

Notes

1. A. Brown. 2015. *The Myth of the Strong Leader: Political Leadership in the Modern Age* (London, UK: The Bodley Head).
2. H.L. Tosi, V.F. Misangyi, A. Fanellid, D.A. Waldmane, and F.J. Yammarino. 2004. "CEO Charisma, Compensation, and Firm Performance," *Leadership Quarterly* 15, no. 3, pp. 405–420.
3. F. Lagerberg. 2015. *The Value of Diversity* (Report) (Chicago, IL: Grant Thornton).

4. H.L. Tosi, V.F. Misangyi, A. Fanellid, D.A. Waldmane, and F.J. Yammarino. 2004. "CEO Charisma, Compensation, and Firm Performance," *Leadership Quarterly*, Op. Cit.

5. J. Rankin. March 6, 2015. "Fewer women leading FTSE firms than men called John." https://www.theguardian.com/business/2015/mar/06/johns-davids-and-ians-outnumber-female-chief-executives-in-ftse-100, (accessed April 6, 2016).

6. J. Kollewe. April 27, 2016. "Women Occupy less than a Quarter of UK Board Positions." https://www.theguardian.com/business/2016/apr/27/women-uk-board-positions-gender-equality-europe, (accessed March 16, 2018).

7. G. Desvaux, S. Devillard-Hoellinger, and P. Baumgarten. 2007. *Women Matter: Gender Diversity, A Corporate Performance Driver* (New York, NY: McKinsey & Company).

8. L. Joy, N.M. Carter, H.M. Wagener, and S. Narayanan. 2007. "The Bottom Line: Corporate Performance and Women's Representation on Boards," *Catalyst*.

9. F. Lagerberg. 2015. *The Value of Diversity* (Report), op.cit.

10. R. Kline. 2014. *The "Snowy White Peaks" of the NHS: A Survey of Discrimination in Governance and Leadership and the Potential Impact on Patient Care in London and England* (London, UK: Middlesex University Research Repository).

11. F. Lagerberg. 2015. *The Value of Diversity* (Report), op.cit.

12. U.S. Glass Ceiling Commission. 1995. *Good for Business: Making Full Use of the Nation's Human Capital: A Fact-finding Report of the Federal Glass Ceiling Commission* (Washington, DC: Government Printing Office), http://digitalcommons.ilr.cornell.edu/key_workplace/116

13. M. Cloyd. September 9, 2013. "Taking a Fresh Look at Board Composition," PricewaterhouseCoopers, Harvard Law School Forum. https://corpgov.law.harvard.edu/2013/09/09/taking-a-fresh-look-at-board-composition/, (accessed May 16, 2018).

14. Chartered Management Institute. February 2018. *21st Century Leaders: Building Employability through Higher Education* (Report) (London, UK: CMI).

15. See e.g., R. Shah. September 25, 2014. "Have You Got Millennial Workforce Expectations All Wrong?" *Forbes*, https://www.forbes.com/

sites/rawnshah/2014/09/25/have-you-got-millennial-workforce-expectations-wrong/2/#6b443a016d3e, (accessed May 16, 2018).

16. S.S. Adams. April 5, 2012. "Why Promoting from Within Usually Beats Hiring from Outside," *Forbes*, http://www.forbes.com/sites/susan-adams/2012/04/05/why-promoting-from-within-usually-beats-hiring-from-outside/#3b6686893fb2, (accessed May 2, 2016).

17. Chartered Management Institute. February 2018. *21st Century Leaders: Building Employability through Higher Education* (Report) (London, UK: CMI), op.cit.

18. K. Wilber. 2007. *A Brief History of Everything*, 2nd ed (Boulder, CO: Shambhala).

19. J. Timpson. 2010. *Upside Down Management* (London, UK: Wiley & Sons).

20. J. Timpson. 2000. *Dear James* (London, UK: Caspian).

21. M. Beard. July 22, 2016. "Follow My Leader," https://www.goodreads.com/author/show/97783.Mary_Beard/blog?page=11, (accessed July 24, 2016).

22. S. Coughlan. September 29, 2015. "Firm 'Hides' University when Recruits Apply," http://www.bbc.co.uk/news/education-34384668, (accessed May 2, 2016).

23. J. Parkinson and M. Smith-Walters. October 26, 2015. *Who, What, Why: What is Name-blind Recruitment?* http://www.bbc.co.uk/news/magazine-34636464, (accessed May 2, 2016).

CHAPTER 4

Brokering Peace
in the War for Talent

Practice peace—change your world

—Prem Rawat

In the same way that it is reputed that "no one ever got fired for buying IBM," I suspect no one ever got fired for agreeing with McKinsey. I'm a bit contrary. In all my years in IT, I never bought IBM, and for quite a while now, I've been screaming "no!" whenever I see the phrase popularized by McKinsey: "The War for Talent"

For a start, I have a problem with the whole war metaphor. I was amused once to read about the "foot soldiers in the battle for peace." There's something ironic in that, and in today's interconnected world, the war metaphor is not helpful.

Organizations that formerly perceived others as "competitors" have had to learn to collaborate. For example, large construction projects may work with more than one firm that might, originally, have been bidding for the contract that the now lead contractor won. They need to collaborate.

Today, more people are working independently as consultants and, through the associate model, supplying their skills to different organizations. The chances are those organizations are competitors, but they'll benefit from sharing the skills of that consultant. With appropriate levels of confidentiality, that consultant will be better as a result of having worked for your competitor and vice versa.

If we see our talented people as a commodity to fight over, it creates a mindset that, while possibly successful in the short term, does long-term damage.

Just because we live and work in a VUCA World doesn't mean that it has to become a battlefield. Indeed, you might argue that the war for talent increases the uncertainty and volatility. It's time for peace. But what might that look like? It certainly looks like an organization that coaches and mentors all its people; where conversations are stretching and challenging without being confrontational; where moving to new projects is seen as an opportunity; and where, despite all the challenges, people feel valued and recognized for their contribution, not overlooked and displaced.

Target Talent

I've managed a lot of teams in my time, and of course, I've had my favorites. The individuals who make the biggest contribution to the team's success, by extension, make me look good. So naturally, I value them. The important thing, though, is how I manage things when either they want to move on or the organization has another project, where I believe their individual or team contribution would be sorely needed.

I hope that I develop and encourage people to move on at the right time; the point where the individual feels it's time to move on is usually too late. Managers are in a better position to notice when a team member is getting bored and their performance is dropping off. I saw part of my role to work out the best point in the arc of performance to start to have the conversation with them about their next role. But if I missed this and they came to me wanting to move on, then it is in everybody's interests to facilitate that willingly and enthusiastically and make it happen as quickly as possible.

If that person leaves my team resentful because I was dragging my feet over their release, then my reputation as a leader and potentially that of the organization we work in is at risk. If they leave thinking well of me and of the organization, then they will tell good stories about us, and potentially, as they broaden and enhance their skills in other companies, they may well return in a more senior role later. And chances are they will assimilate back in more easily than a brand new hire would.

There's a financial benefit to this approach. In 2010[1] and 2011,[2] two authors highlighted the financial value of promoting from within the existing talent pool in the organization, rather than paying lip service to developing talent and then recruiting expensive and poorly performing outsiders.

How often have you worked in organizations where a new project has come along that requires the brightest and the best to make it a success? The word goes out, and managers offer up someone for the role. All too often, existing managers see this as an opportunity to get rid of the "difficult" or "awkward" members of their team, rather than supporting the new project's future success. The ideal is to resource these important projects with the best people; if it makes your organization more successful, then it will have a positive impact on everyone.

I worked for a boss once who was so frustrated by the unwillingness of his managers to let their best team members move around that he called us all into a conference room one day. He was standing at the front with two big jars. One contained the names of the key people in the organization. The other contained some vacancies on important projects that we were unable to fill. He started to pull pieces of paper from each jar, matching a random person to random job vacancy. I remember watching this and thinking, "Hmm, they're going to struggle in that role, but it could be interesting. We should do that."

I was fully on board with this novel approach, until the name of one of my team was pulled out, when my reaction was, "Are you kidding? They could never do that and anyway I need them!" After "filling" about six vacancies, our boss stopped and told us, of course, he wasn't going to make those moves happen. But the unsaid subtext was if we didn't contribute, he might well repeat the exercise for real.

That was probably the point in my own learning when I shifted my own way of thinking. My unconscious bias was so blatantly, and publicly, exposed that I had to acknowledge my own part in the suppression of talent. Another benefit of moving the so-called best people on to new projects is that it gives great opportunities for other people in your organization to shine. You may have missed their talents because they were overshadowed.

The gardening world offers a great analogy. You have a plant that's alive, but you can see it's not thriving. Yes, you water and feed it, but your senses tell you it's not quite enough. Sometimes, repotting the plant in a bigger container is the solution to revitalize it. Now, I'm not saying our employees are plants, but the analogy holds.

I was working with an organization, supporting them to create a good succession planning approach. We did all the usual things: identifying who was suitable for the promotion and in what sort of time frame, looking at the jobs that they may be best suited to going to, and analyzing the roles in the organization to determine which were the critical ones where we absolutely need to have a good plan.

Additionally, we identified roles that would be ideal development opportunities for people with the talent, potentially, to fill the critical or more senior roles. The people currently occupying those roles would not necessarily be looking to move and their roles weren't mission critical. But what it meant was we could create some great opportunities by moving people on. In some cases, the long-term inhabitants of those roles were happy where they were and resisted being moved on. However, many did eventually admit that having been "repotted," they too had found benefits in an otherwise unexpected and unplanned move.

This takes a combination of some forward thinking and, perhaps, deep breaths and clenching of teeth. However, when we can see the advantages of moving people around in the organization, more people might sign up to the notion.

Support Career Development Outside the Organization

But what if I said you should move a person onto a different organization? I was once responsible for creating a pool of internal coaches. One of the huge advantages of an internal coaching panel, using managers trained as coaches, is that you can break down silos across the organization.

A secondment opportunity is another way of achieving a wider "real world" view. Investing in this kind of development is a clear win/win. Not only are the coach-like managers better leaders because they have the skills, but where they volunteered to coach people across departments, both parties benefit as well. If a person from engineering is coaching someone from marketing, both departments get to learn more about each other and, through the coaching skills, build better trust, rapport, and communications.

Through networking, I had come across two or three other organizations that had done the same. I suggested it might be a good idea if we shared our coaches across organizations. We'd see how different organizations operated, and we might bring back some great learning into our organization. Sadly, my seniors were terrified at the thought of our best people being poached as a result of another organization finding out, through coaching them, that they were quite good. I may not have won that argument, but it helped me see the fear that arises from the notions of competition and the "war for talent." All these examples, and the lost opportunities to go alongside them, stemmed from thinking that we are in a battle.

And I understand that the immediate, tactical, and operational priorities mean that it's hard for people to see the strategic benefit of wider experiences. But at a time when organizations are calling for greater innovation and creativity, new and different experiences are powerful ways to develop those skills.

Talent as a "Finite" Resource

Another, subtler message implicit in that phrase is that talent is a finite resource. A bit like fossil fuels, one day it will run out, so let's squeeze the maximum out of people for the short time they're with us. It's simply not true. If we nurture talent well, it's more like a renewable resource.

We see this attitude in the world of soccer. In the UK, football clubs, driven by the need for short-term success, are more likely to go into the external market and pay increasingly inflated fees for established stars. The alternative, of investing in young local talent, is seen as too dangerous in the short life spans of the managers. And it plays to the fans who get more excited when some big name signs for their club, as opposed to seeing someone rise through from the youth academy and taking pride in the investment in more local talent.

If we see talent as being a finite resource, then, of course, we will go to war to hang onto our best or to steal from the opposition. Hanging onto our best is not a great strategy, and I would also argue that "stealing" from the opposition can be counterproductive.

First, the evidence[3] suggests that well-developed, homegrown leaders are more successful than those parachuted in, especially at the top of the organization, the CEO or the COO. And remember, you already have a pool of underdeveloped, untapped women; people from diverse cultural backgrounds; and younger people, all being overlooked because they don't fit the traditional paradigm.

Secondly, if those external, sought-after individuals do get lured to you through some promising package, then you have created a mindset of them being a commodity that can be secured by the highest bidder. How loyal are they likely to be?

The headhunting industry relies on churn. While they're promising you the exclusive on a highly valuable external hire, they're scouting around your organization and promising the moon and stars to your existing talent, who may feel under-recognized and undervalued. There is likely to be an impact on the existing people in your organization: the role that gets filled by this imported star is likely to be one that people saw as their next step. This makes them much more vulnerable to the lure of the headhunter the next time they get that call. So, you have simultaneously stirred up unrest with your existing team, created a mercenary attitude, and potentially, hired a failure. All because you got seduced by the idea that talent is finite and therefore you had better get your hands on some soon.

A much better strategy is to grow your own. It is, as a side benefit, quite likely to be a cheaper option as well as being more effective.

The FortonD^4 (4D) Model

We recommend four steps to systematically optimize your existing and potential leader and manager resources: define, discover, develop, and deploy. In our Organizational Development (OD) or Learning and Development (L&D) consulting assignments, this is our typical starting place for exploring what our clients already have in place, before we recommend new initiatives.

D^1: Define

While, by now, it may seem obvious, it is vital that you clearly define exactly what the talent is you are trying to grow. You need to look at what the leadership needs are in the organization right now and also be planning for the future. Most organizations will be moving and changing quite quickly, and so anticipating the future need rather than just replicating existing styles is important.

Indeed, it may not be leadership you are short of; perhaps, there is technical or professional style of leadership that is important. The role of the thought leader in inspiring creativity and innovation in your organization will be quite different from, and complementary to, the leadership required to deliver your new vision or strategy.

D^2: Discover

Before embarking on some expensive wholesale development program, it's worth looking deeply at what talents and skills you already have in the organization. Sheep dipping is useful only if the whole flock has got disease, and given today's freedom through blended and self-directed learning, it makes sense to personalize and target the learning investment.

While targeted leadership development programs have their place, you may find you have some great internal skills that can be shared, for example, by developing the mentoring skills in your older or more experienced leaders.

The sense of "legacy" and "giving something back" is typically strong in people who have grown their career through the organization. Mentoring is a powerful win/win because it shows you value both parties. It grows confidence, builds loyalty, and helps you discover hidden talents in the organization.

In any sizeable organization, you're going to find pockets of different team or departmental cultures with different talents across the organization, so it makes sense to see diversity as a resource and find ways to tap into it.

D^3: Develop

Formal training programs based on a clear definition of need ("define," above) and existing potential ("discover") still have a vital role to play. Yet there are other alternatives to consider. Putting a team together to tackle a strategic project is a great way for them to learn about leadership, especially if they are facilitated in ways that mean they genuinely try new ideas and learn, rather than just approaching the project in the way they would have done anyway.

Coaching and mentoring, from either internal or external people, is often rated as one of the most useful interventions by the people being developed. I mentioned earlier that a particularly effective way to make best use of all resources is to train leaders and managers to be more coach-like. Creating an in-house coaching team, a subset of those people willing to carry out coaching and mentoring roles, is another valuable resource. You can also train them to a higher level as coaches, which has a number of advantages.

Your leaders will be better for knowing how and when to deploy a coach approach. You will have an internal pool of coaches that, while not entirely replacing external coaches, bring some cost savings. You can clearly measure the impacts and return on investment (ROI), which can help improve your management of external coaching services.

As a consequence, people will be developed through being coached. Most importantly, because the coach–coachee relationship will be across different teams, you will start to break down some of the silo mentality that typically pervades complex organizations. The design of the development intervention is crucial.

I recently completed an advanced driving course. I'd like to pretend this was solely driven by my interest in driving, but I must confess that a gentle nudge from a driver-awareness course, offered to people who have been caught speeding, was part of my motivation. *Mea culpa*! Now, I really enjoyed the advanced driving lessons, and I would heartily recommend the course to anyone.

However, I went through some of the challenges that face adults who have to learn new skills. My instructor was great: a really expert driver who volunteers his time for free to take people like me out for a couple of hours and help improve their driving. His style was fine, a good mix of encouragement and pointing out places to improve, but I still had a problem with having my mistakes pointed out to me.

I tried to work out why. I just felt stupid: I'm an adult, surely I should know everything? I found myself arguing back, justifying why I chose the gear I did, or why the speed really was right. What I learned from this is how important it is to get feedback right. To create a supportive environment for learning.

I was also going through that phase of conscious incompetence, trying to change the way I approached roundabouts, getting the deceleration, the speed, the gear, and the steering all just right. As a long-term driver, I'd been doing this unconsciously for years, but bringing awareness back to the surface and trying to adjust meant, initially, I was getting it wrong more often than right.

So the development phase includes careful design, blending the learning methods, peer support, coaching and mentoring, as well as positive feedback approaches.

D⁴: Deploy

Whichever routes you choose to develop your people, it's key that you then give them opportunities to apply their newfound skills so they continue to learn and grow. Providing leadership opportunities means designing in work shadowing, opportunities to "act up," for example, by attending meetings with the necessary decision-making powers or undertaking holiday cover at the senior level.

All these opportunities rely on the willingness and ability of senior people to trust and respect junior people and to delegate and properly hand off tasks to them. When well organized and prepared, these leadership opportunities offer greater stability and continuity for the organization.

The Final Leadership Taboo

In the 21st century, the notion of leadership from younger people is one of the most challenging concepts. We pay lip service to encouraging leadership development in women or supporting people from diverse cultural backgrounds to develop their skills, but leadership from younger people feels like the last taboo in this field.

There's an often repeated maxim that we reward people for their increasing experience and role longevity. But what if that's not 20 years of experience, but just 1 year's experience repeated 20 times? When we shift recognition and reward systems away from annual pay rises (which reward loyalty but little else) to rewarding technical leadership, based on skills and contribution, factors such as age cease to matter.

Recognizing technical leadership has the added advantage of not promoting people unsuitable to people management into those types of leadership roles. When looking to recruit, or when looking to move people internally, there is a growing body of evidence that a more effective approach can be to recruit a home team or reuse an existing team, rather than trying to build from a disparate group of individuals.

We've already shown that the impact of a single individual, especially at the more senior levels, is often overrated; the stories of the organizations "saved" by hero leader are legion but not entirely true. If you have a team of people who have been working on a project that has come to an end, then reassigning them as a team has the advantage that they already know how to operate well as a team that can cut down the time it takes to reach peak performance. Equally, while logistically more complex, bringing in an existing successful team from outside could work in the same way.

When intelligent people lack drive and challenge in their role, they look around for it; if they don't find opportunities to stretch themselves in their current roles, they often leave the organization—at great cost to employers. The cost of replacing lost employees is fourfold[4]: "stars" bought in from outside tend to cost 18 percent more than their replacement, and there may be additional costs in raising pay for the team members who receive the new leader. They are crucial to ensuring the new hire gets up to speed, and there is an overall decline in performance during this period. At the end of all this cost in time, effort, and extra money, the new star is 61 percent more likely to be let go than internally developed leaders.

This waste in talent and resources is costly and unnecessary, as well as improving performance and return on assets by filling the leadership gap with a more inclusive and diverse pool of leadership talent, there is still an opportunity to achieve value, even if people—such as the young rising stars—are (temporarily) leaving the organization.

Now's the time to drop this war analogy. Create abundant leadership in your organization, start using the talent you have, and stop paying the price for waste.

Worksheet: Stimulus Questions

In this chapter we look at the options of recruiting leaders and managers from outside the organization versus identifying, developing, and supporting in-house talent to grow. Before the 4D™ method can be applied, it's worth thinking about how the organization works today, in terms of recruitment, retention, and leadership development.

Survey Your Colleagues

Ask, "On a scale of 1 to 10 (where 1 is low and 10 is high), how good is the succession planning process at spotting talent in this organization?"

Targeting Talented People

How well does the organization culture support the easy flow of talent?

Coaching Culture

How might a coaching culture better support individuals, teams, and performance?

Organizational Reputation

What's the impression of your organization that you want people who leave to take with them into the wider world?

Radical Thinking

What radical change to your recruitment system would have the biggest positive impact?

The 4D Method

- Define
- Discover
- Develop
- Deploy

Notes

1. B. Groysberg. 2010. *Chasing Stars: The Myth of Talent and the Portability of Performance* (Princeton, NJ: Princeton University Press).
2. M. Bidwell. September 2011. "Paying More to Get Less: The Effects of External Hiring versus Internal Mobility." *Administrative Science Quarterly* 56, no. 3, pp. 369–407.
3. B. Groysberg. 2010. *Chasing Stars: The Myth of Talent and the Portability of Performance* and M. Bidwell. 2011. "Paying More to Get Less: The Effects of External Hiring versus Internal Mobility," op.cit.
4. R. Shah. September 25, 2014. *Have You Got Millennial Workforce Expectations All Wrong?* Quoting the work of Prof. Matthew Bidwell.

CHAPTER 5

Mining for Gold

In most cases being a good boss means hiring talented people and then getting out of their way.

—Tina Fey

It's the backbone of every successful Hollywood film plot: the mysterious outsider who comes with great promise to save the day, with eyes hidden beneath a wide-brimmed hat and collar turned up to add to the mystique; dramatic music rises to a crescendo in the background. It's an enticing image, with the promise of a shortcut to better leadership. Someone will just stroll into your town and put things right.

It's easy to see why people fall for the myth of the hero leader. This plot gets played out daily as organizations up and down the land interview their candidates and listen to the alluring promise of a potential hire. This chapter explores the allure of the outsider: the notion that it's automatically better to bring talent into the organization from outside than to develop the talent that's already available.

This myth risks hiring people who, while successful in another context, fail to live up to their promise and flounder in the new environment. It also risks alienating good people who are hungry for the chance to stretch and develop their potential. It addresses the "familiarity breeds contempt" assumption and challenges readers to see their people from a fresh angle (beginners' mind) and to find ways to tap into their latent talent.

We explore the need for organizations to ensure that the "induction" process lasts longer than the first week—and indeed starts before that. In pilot phases people get the chance to try out new roles in a supportive environment.

And, because context is everything, the solutions may not be either/or decisions, rather a blend of people. We encourage you to mine for gold. This isn't just about decisions made in the HR department. This chapter is about actions that every manager can take to improve the success of their team and prepare for the development of everyone in it. Understanding that this is a shared task makes everyone's life easier.

Most employers are aware that new recruits come with costs attached. Weighing up the costs with the potential benefits is an important activity in the "Discover" step of the leadership and organization development process. It's also connected to the importance of identifying benefits and impacts, so that everyone knows what "ROI" looks like in terms of the investments you're making in growing the organization's leadership capabilities.

And it's not just the costs of CV sifting or setting up assessment centers, interview panels, and reference checking. It takes up to a year for new staff to achieve optimum productivity and costs an average of £25,000 per new employee.[1]

For sales recruitment the payback time can be longer: 18 months to 2 years is not uncommon. And yet employers expect much faster returns, often without putting in the support structures that contribute toward successful outcomes.

In 2017, the UK CMI[2] stated: "The UK currently has an estimated 2.4m accidental and unskilled managers, promoted into leadership roles because of their functional expertise but left to sink or swim when it comes to management."

Evidence started back in 2010[3] and 2011[4] when two authors highlighted the financial value of promoting from within the existing talent pool in organizations. Organizations paid lip service to developing talent and then recruited expensive and poor-performing outsiders. These practices also encourage wage inflation, spurred on by the people, who most stand to gain from parachuting in new talent, earning commission from the headhunting process.

So, helping everyone in the organization to discover, value, and develop the talent around them is an important task, not just one for the HR department working in isolation. Every manager can improve their team performance now by taking these steps.

In the film *The Hudsucker Proxy,*[5] there's a fast-moving scene where the lead actor is introduced to the company policies around pay in a series of rapid explanations, each one ending with the conclusion: "Do this, or they'll dock ya!" Exaggerated for humorous effect, it reflects the impact of new ways of working. It can feel overwhelming when you're being introduced to a new environment, starting work for a new employer. The additional costs of external recruits are threefold:

1. The potential to create wage inflation
2. The costs of head-hunter commissions
3. The cost of time taken to reach optimum effectiveness.

Unless the payback can be shown to be of real benefit to the organization, this effort risks being a waste of time and money.

Now We Are Going to Contradict Ourselves. . .

This does not mean that recruiting and promoting from within is always the right solution. The threat from too much of the same-group thinking can create the "not invented here" syndrome, where the in-house solution is the only solution.

There are too many examples, particularly in the IT world, where budgets have been blown on hobby projects, when a turnkey solution already exists. Stories of slowly evolving projects (for example, to bring many disparate systems into a single process) have been overtaken by smaller, more flexible solutions.[6] This narrow thinking shuts down the wider range of alternatives and focuses on delivering the solution (or should that be "THE solution"). This focus on delivery is admirable; however, it works best once a range of options have been explored—and openly discussed without barriers to success.

This is where a new, less subjective person can help others see things from a fresh angle, with a beginner's mind set, and tap into the pool of talent.

Ways need to be found to both develop people from within the organization and create the optimum conditions for new hires. This is what mining for gold is about. It is about looking for what works and identifying areas of change—with the goal of supporting staff, new and old, to be successful in their roles.

While supporting a major public hospital complex to prepare for change, we interviewed a range of staff from senior consultants to back-office workers. Given the rate of change in that high-achieving organization, the discovery step included a review of the existing talent development processes. We found many examples of dedicated staff, finding new ways to improve patient care and introducing new ideas at the same time—ideas to ensure accurate, accessible patient records available on demand and to share learning from across the world and root out ineffective, out-of-date practices.

Yet, one overriding theme was that people were introduced to new ideas in a formal, lecture-style setting, but that the support stopped there. When these processes were taken into the real world of a busy hospital, they broke down under the reality of everyday life. But rather than evaluating the induction processes, it was assumed that the talent selection process has chosen "the wrong people."

The cost to the organization was measured in terms of sickness and absenteeism (adapting to new environments is stressful) and staff turnover. Another issue arose: people reverted to their old ways of doing things because that was what they knew worked for them. Some leaders gave "special dispensation" to failing individuals and teams—because they thought they were being helpful.

In one department, the managers themselves distrusted the new systems and continued to use the old, manual system as well as the new automated process. This had the impact of duplicating work for their team members, whose training in the new system was discounted, which slowed the whole system down.

A key element of mining for gold is to discover the optimum working environments for the individual, the team, and the organization. It's about planning for skills application, not just classroom learning. It's about seeing line managers as part of the solution. It's about making the link between the individual and the environment in which they work.

Remove Structural Barriers to Optimize Performance

In another hospital, the building itself contributed to the separation between team members, such that processes needed to be duplicated, even triplicated. When dealing with the laboratory samples from very sick people, this was recognized as unacceptable. Speed and first-time accuracy were vital, so mining for gold included finding ways to have a single point of contact between the wards and the laboratories.

When we explored the issues, we found ourselves talking to people who were individually highly talented, sociable, and intelligent. The challenge was that they were locked in their own silos and had little awareness of what other people were—or were not—doing. The gold we uncovered was that they shared a passion for high standards. They recognized and valued it in their colleagues. They saw the commitment in the staff bringing the precious samples and were unanimous in wanting to work together to make the processes seamless.

Creating an environment for success increases the chance of successful induction, reducing the costs of introducing new people into the system.

When Does It Make Sense to Bring In Outsiders?

Going back to the first step in the FortonD^4 steps, the most obvious time to bring in external talent is when what is defined as needed is something very different from what is there today: when it is time for transformation.

When organizations need to go into "turnaround" mode, requiring a focused, pacesetting style of leadership, the "Discover" step of mining for gold will tell you whether or not using existing leadership talent is going to be credible. A turnaround strategy requires a ruthless focus on a small number of vital priorities that deliver against the organization's turnaround goals. This means that other activities will be of less importance in that bigger picture.

A turnaround strategy is easier to implement when the leader has the position of an "objective outsider" rather than that of a longstanding team member. Don't forget that this doesn't negate the value of the "business as usual" operational managers and leaders.

One client organization had such a focus on bringing in an outsider to turn the company around and set it up for sale that they failed to notice the levels of complaints against current contracts or to notice the loss of key business. Knowing who is best placed to keep the organization steady, while major changes are happening around, is vital. Mining for gold in this instance means knowing the following:

- What leadership the organization needs on the operational side ("Define" step)?
- What specific behaviors might be different between the strategic and operational elements?
- Who already has the potential to deliver those leadership behaviors?

That flotation was canceled by the way.

Organizational Maturity

Sometimes it's necessary to bring in a leader whose preferred leadership style is different from the prevailing culture. When an organization needs to do something very different in order to be more successful in the future, an outsider is likely to be better placed to deliver that difference. Examples include start-ups that are reaching a more stable, mature phase in their development, or slow, consensus-led organizations that need to address significant change toward rapid implementation and shift the culture first.

Prevailing organizational culture is closely linked to the willingness, or otherwise, to change. It is also closely linked, emotionally, to values. It was the shared values and ethos of the laboratory team that drove the willingness to change rapidly. Once they had seen what was happening, and the impact on patients, the will to change was there. Selecting a leader that appreciates the prevailing organizational values and yet will still lead the shift toward the needed organizational culture is vital.

Mining for gold is not just about discovering untapped leadership potential in people; it's also about ensuring that leadership development is closely aligned to cultural development. While any organization can create posters with inspiring vision statements and post them up in their foyer, the impact is nullified if staff have no say in the values statements. It takes leadership to cocreate values and explore their meaning with the team.

Communications teams often work from a belief that for the values to be taken on board, they need to be, literally, writ large. Yet, in terms of impact, the size of the letters is inversely proportional to the cultural buy-in to those values. Leadership that supports cultural buy-in actively contributes to the shifts needed in that organization's development.

Mining for Gold Creates the Cultural Environment

The pathology team in the hospital was physically separated by being on different floors in the building. They were brought together by developing a single system that everyone bought into. But visible structural barriers aren't the only ones; the internal, invisible, beliefs—notably about "ways of working"—can be just as potent barriers as stairs or lab layouts.

Another role in mining for gold is to have those exploratory conversations to

- Discover, and evaluate, the prevailing organizational culture
- Support honest conversations about that culture
- Uncover the organization's lived values (as distinct from the "handed down" values statements)
- Discover the preexisting innate talent within the organization
- Identify the touch points or working environment contexts likely to support or hinder success

Mining for gold is about creating the right environment for successful recruitment and retention. And success can be measured in many ways.

Tim Gallwey is famous for his "Inner Game" book series, dealing with our inner beliefs and attitudes. Gallwey's equation[7] for achieving potential sums up this area: "Performance equals Potential minus Interference." To improve performance, it's important to remove the interference: whether that's internal or external. This, in itself, unlocks a person's potential.

So, if people have beliefs about the way they work that prevent optimum performance, the challenge might be to provide leadership that removes those beliefs and thus the barriers, freeing people from old ways of working to achieve at their best.

The challenge is how you do that. Is it better to start by addressing peoples' weaknesses? Or move them out of their comfort zone first? Or support their confidence by building on their track record of success to date?

The topic of individual development will be covered more fully in step three, the "Develop" section of this book. But let's look at other ways to remove interference from people's working lives. The prevailing culture is a great opportunity to create an environment in which people can be successful.

The Way We Do Things Around Here

What we mean by the "prevailing organizational culture" is more than the official story. Each department will have an unwritten code about the "way we do things around here." These are the shared beliefs about the best way of working, expressed through people's behaviors. These beliefs, and ways of working, can act as enablers or interference to people and teams.

The emotional intelligence work of Dulewicz and Higgs[8] describes these in two categories: the "Rational-brain Focus" of strategies, goals, and objectives and the "Emotional-brain Focus" of vision, mission, and values. A marketing or sales department will have a very different set of goals and objectives (such as "relationship building" as a priority) than a finance department ("accuracy"). The challenge is to integrate the higher-defined needs of the organization, against the ways of working within departments, and align those invisible, emotional elements.

Helping people see how their department's goals, targets, and objectives play into the bigger picture is a key part of that integration. It removes barriers to performance because people feel valued and successful when they know their contribution counts—and precisely how it counts.

Supporting honest conversations about the prevailing culture and values, in the light of the defined organizational purpose, and in service of stability where necessary, is also a key part of that integration. The priority is to preserve existing values where they add value to the organization and demonstrate this as a conscious choice.

Leadership and Taking New Directions

Likewise, if the decision is to shift away from an existing value, it also needs to be both conscious and explicit. Leaders need to dig deep and draw on their communication skills to facilitate this shift. An honest conversation is itself a values-driven exchange, and while people may not agree with the decisions made, or the route chosen, the clear explanation for the new direction is itself an honest position on which people can agree to disagree.

An example might be where a young, entrepreneurial company recognizes the need to shift toward a more stable state, perhaps bringing in policies and procedures to ensure consistency when rapid growth is happening. Chances are the existing teams won't feel comfortable with this shift toward a more "rigid" or confined environment.

Increased bureaucracy, such as booking your holidays 3 months in advance, to make sure there's cover to deal with customers and projects might be perceived as rigid or stultifying creativity. Addressing the cultural and values-related issues in this way is particularly important for the humanitarian clients for whom we work, often necessary when, in times of straitened circumstances, budgets have to be cut and efforts focused in a particular way.

Many such organizations are also being called upon to be more transparent, particularly in the way they handle and spend donor monies. This means that just delivering financial information is no longer enough. Access to high-quality, up-to-date information and presentations that show the flow between money out and projects delivered are vital to the donor confidence.

These requirements lead the staff to question why what was previously "good enough performance" is no longer enough. A values-based conversation, aligned to the organization's goals, is a necessity. This is more than paying lip service to an organization's charter or values statement. It requires an approach to leadership that succeeds in engaging and involving the staff in how these values play out—in their workplace context.

Mining for gold in current team members often requires an attitudinal shift in line managers and colleagues. It's easy to fall into the rut of looking for what's wrong in someone rather than catching them doing things right. The mining for gold process applies equally to the hire of external talent, such that, when it's needed, every external hire can be supported to be most successful.

Recruiters often talk about the "right fit" to the organization and to the team; what often happens is that this is more about "recruiting people in my image" than real cultural "fit." Mining for gold as a process of discovery is about uncovering what a new hire can really bring—as distinct from them presenting what you want to see. It's not hard for an astute interviewee to see what's going on over on the other side of the table and play to their audience.

It's also possible to anticipate true "alignment"—at a deep level—long before the interview stage through situational profiling. One approach is to offer online situational judgment assessments, even before the CV-sifting process.

You can identify people likely to fit the organizational profile and reject those whose values really don't fit. Or, if you're looking for someone whose approach meets the need of the change, you're better placed to consciously recruit someone outside of the current culture.

This is a practical way to filter people in or out by their attitude, not just aptitude. CVs, assessment centers, and interviews can all come later. One word of caution though: if the organization needs this kind of cultural shift, whether it's the rapid turnaround of the organization or the maturing of an entrepreneurial start-up business, one leader alone won't be enough.

I've seen too many solo, would-be hero leaders fail because they don't have the support around them. This is why abundant leadership is vital. You need a team of leaders, fully on board, to make transformational organizational shifts. People who feel alone are less likely to succeed. Look at women at the board level; where there is a group of women sufficient to create comradeship and critical mass, success happens.

A study of corporate boards[9] found it takes three women to really change the dynamic in the board room. A lone woman is made to feel she represents the "woman's point of view and can be left out of decision making discussions and even social gatherings." Adding a second woman helps. But the "magic seems to occur when three or more women serve on a board together," the study concludes.

> Suddenly, women are no longer seen as outsiders and their influence on the content and process of discussions increases substantially.

> And, by mining for gold, you can discover who in your organization has the attitude and capacity to work well together and deliver the type of leadership you need.

Relentless Exploration, Simple Steps

Key to the discovery step is the need to mine for gold. The miners in the 1849 Gold Rush had simple tools to pan for nuggets of gold in the rivers and streams of California and the persistence to keep looking. In the FortonD^4 method, mining for gold is relentlessly exploring what's already available to the team and the organization before recruiting from outside.

This may take a change of attitude, and fresh thinking, to be reminded of the resources that already exist, identifying what's untapped and then evaluating what's really needed. It takes broad exploration rather than rushing into action and narrow thinking. It also takes realism, and yes, sometimes the right answer might well be that the external hire really is needed.

Worksheet: Stimulus Questions

This chapter is about digging a little deeper in the discovery phase, looking at the strategic needs of the organization, and, at the same time, maintaining business as usual. This means discovering the leadership talents and qualities needed for both types of role and uncovering the abundance of talent that already exists.

It also means looking at the culture and values of the organization and whether they're fit for purpose in the future: whether that's a turnaround situation or moving toward organizational maturity, such as from an entrepreneurial environment to one of more controlled growth.

These questions link your "define" phase to the deeper levels of discovery:

Recap the Need from the "define" Step

- What are the defined needs of the organization in terms of strategic leadership, that is, the future direction of the organization?
- What are the defined leadership needs in terms of "business as usual?"

Optimize Your Induction Programs

- How are you supporting people to be successful in new roles in terms of induction?
- What's working in your induction programs?
- What needs to be different?

Review the Organization Values and Culture

- Which values, that are important to people today, need to shift to deliver the future organizational vision?
- What conversations do leaders need to have with their teams to support cultural change and transformation?

Mine for Gold

- What tools do you already have, to identify the gold that already exists in your organization?
- What more do you need to meet these needs?

Notes

1. Oxford Economics. 2014. "The Cost of Brain Drain: Understanding the Financial Impact of Staff Turnover" (Report for Unum), https://www.oxfordeconomics.com
2. Leadership Centre. n.d. *Leadership for Change* (London, UK: Chartered Management Institute).

3. B. Groysberg. 2010. *Chasing Stars: The Myth of Talent and the Portability of Performance* (Princeton, NJ: Princeton University Press).

4. M. Bidwell. 2011. "Paying More to Get Less: The Effects of External Hiring versus Internal Mobility." *Administrative Science Journal* 56, no. 3, pp. 369–407.

5. Cohen Bros. 1994. *The Hudsucker Proxy* (Burbank, CA: Warner Bros).

6. R. Syal. 2013. "Abandoned NHS IT System has Cost £10bn So Far," *Guardian*.

7. W.T. Gallwey. 1999. *The Inner Game of Work* (New York, NY: Random House).

8. V. Dulewicz and M. Higgs. 2000. "Emotional intelligence—A review and evaluation study." *Journal of Managerial Psychology* 15, no. 4, pp. 341–72.

9. V.W. Kramer, A.M. Konrad, and S. Erkut. 2006. *Critical Mass and Corporate Boards: Why Three or More Women Enhance Governance* (Wellesley, MA: Wellesley Centers for Women).

CHAPTER 6

Filling the Vase

The old adage "people are our greatest asset" is wrong; "the right people are your greatest asset" is more accurate.

—Jim Collins

The central myth of the hero is of the lone man—that it's the work of a single person to achieve the goal. Yet, think of every major achievement with a single hero figure at the front, and you'll find a team behind the scenes, playing their part.

- The round-the-world yachtsmen and women
- Space station astronauts
- Sportspeople lifting their trophies—whether that's at Wimbledon or at an F1 event

The narrative has been changing recently, and today's heroes are better at acknowledging the contribution of the team. And, of course, in some cases, they *do* go out and deliver single-handedly.

We're certainly not trying to dismiss or belittle the quality of what they achieve. It's just that the lone hero myth creates a number of problems. It values only people at the top of the organization or those who are most prominent. The people who represent the "face" of your organization. The people who speak convincingly but their words don't always match their actions. These are the people likely to attract the biggest pay raises and bonuses. Yet, their success is dependent on the people who work for them and around them.

As we say, it's changing—look at what happens when a tennis star announces a change in their coach. We're getting better at recognizing the work that goes on behind the scenes. But every time a leader achieves a plaudit without acknowledging others, it devalues the team effort—the technical experts, the researchers, the number crunchers. The people who bring the tea or clean the offices. Each one of them, in their own way, contributes to the overall success.

It creates and perpetuates an image of what a "leader" looks like and how they should behave. And there's another problem to this model. People believe, rightly or wrongly, that they should work in the style of their boss or of the most successful salesperson, whether or not those are the behaviors the organization needs to be successful.

And, because our leadership role models are more likely to be older, male, and from the prevailing monoculture, what worked in the past may not be the best leadership model to develop for the future. In today's connected world, leadership is much more about relationships and sociability. It's about the ability to say the right thing, even in tough situations, and to encourage collaboration, even among the most competitive people.

In this next step in the discovery phase, it helps to put a name to the value people bring, such that everyone gets to share in the glory. It's about the whole organization developing a diversity mind set and really getting to know the team. Whatever else you do in your talent discovery phase, it's time to break the out-of-date links between the hero myth, the recognition, and the reward system, and focus on what works. Most importantly, it's time to celebrate consistency.

Zero-Sum Game: Winners and Losers

It was pay review time once again and my client was feeling under pressure to name the top performers. He was also recommended to lose one of his most-valued team members. "She's the person who's always there in the background," he told me. "She has the back of every member of the team."

We talked about the story of filling the vase—thinking about his "big rocks": the people who made the most noise around the department; pulled off a couple of coups now and then; and had a strong, and mainly positive, presence in the team.

We talked about how those "big characters" had a negative effect, on occasions, by stifling debate or talking down different perspectives. Then he talked about the smaller pebbles. The people who, day in and day out, do the research, crunch the numbers, and sort out the supplier contracts to make the rest of the organization look good.

And finally, we discussed how the two administrative support staff members held it all together. "You don't see them getting the glory, but you do see them being thanked, every day, by someone in the team who's grateful for their efforts." By getting rid of someone, just because they will save money in the short term or they don't appear to be the same quality as your "star" performers, is a false economy.

This is what we mean by a "zero-sum" game. It's a race to the bottom. It may have spectacular winners, but it will also create unnecessary losers. Sadly, it's a mistake many organizations make: retaining the managers with aspirations to work on the most exciting projects and raise their profile as strategic leaders, while gutting the teams that deliver the systematic (often labeled as "routine") tasks.

There's a lot of hot air written on the topic of embracing and valuing diversity, and at its heart, there's simply a deep appreciation for the value of difference. Because difference brings new thinking and new ways of looking at old things, it shines light on the commonplace in new ways. And it delivers the whole, not just the shiniest parts.

We're not just talking about gender or cultural diversity here, which bring huge value to the workplace; we're also talking about the way different people approach the same challenge. Exploring those different approaches can bring value, rather than relying on the standard "we've always done it this way" response.

Being reminded of peoples' value and acknowledging their value are two important steps in the discovery phase. And there's a third step: identifying consistency. There's a vital role for line managers in this phase because while it's possible for psychometric tools to profile against the desired people and pick out those with the highest potential, it's also known for people to respond to those assessment tools by thinking about what the employer wants to hear.

Observed behavior is a much better predictor of how people will behave in future situations. Most importantly, we can see people behaving in a variety of situations and identify what consistent traits they show. This links to the notion of recruiting and developing for attitude, not just for current or future aptitude.

If we train and develop people well enough, they can learn new skills and behaviors. It's a much longer process to develop peoples' relationship skills and sociability. Picking people most likely to thrive and help people around them to thrive is an important task because it's an investment in the whole culture, not just in the individual.

To pick up on the example of thanking the team, the willingness to acknowledge others is a strength; it builds rapport, relationships, and better communications. It demonstrates that much-desired trait of "vulnerability," because we can't do everything alone, and acknowledging others starts with acknowledging our own skill gaps. Doing it occasionally is great, but those people who regularly acknowledge and thank others are consistently building the team.

And consistent team building has a much higher value than the one-off "let's go tenpin bowling and call it team building" approaches. That's not to say you don't have fun together as a team. This first step is important because it's in our nature to forget the contributions people make, especially if they are low key. It's also important to pinpoint exactly why they're important contributors—or seem to be important.

Sometimes just going through this process, as a one-off exercise, helps to nail the value people bring. It can also help bring out the values that contribute to the overall team success.

- The person who sorts out the customer account queries
- The person who makes sure the numbers add up
- The people who bring consistency
- Or those who bring "off-the-wall" creativity

The right environment is vital too. Some peoples' strengths come to the fore when they operate in a particular arena. Defining the situations where someone has a strength and uses it at the optimum will also help identify their value to the team. The Gallup[1] definition of a strength is consistent high performance in a particular way. It's not just the doing; they also note the sense of fulfilment that people experience when they play to their strengths in the workplace.

You'd rightly expect them to have evidence as a research company, and they claim that

- People who use their strengths every day are six times more likely to be engaged on the job.
- Teams that focus on their strengths are 12.5 percent more productive.
- People succeed when they focus on what they do best.

In high-pressure situations, for example, some people are great at motivating the team through a particular challenge. That same person might fail to demonstrate the ability to deal with day-to-day operational issues, leading to a buildup of routine tasks. Or they might be unable to delegate, costing wasted time if they're not available to complete a task.

Discover Strengths at the Individual Level

If Chapter 5 was about recognizing the untapped potential in the company generally, now we're talking about really getting to know individuals for their talents, strengths, and potential. Seek out and discover the people in the team who show consistency, with concrete examples, and it's easier to put a value to it—even those people whose consistency theme is variety!

And this is where the diversity adds such great value. Let the people who are good at the day-to-day operations shine in that area. If that's their strength, let them deliver. It's a waste of everyone's time, money, and effort to try and make someone's weakness into a strength. Yes, you might want to neutralize any de-railing behaviors, so that everyone in the team is operating to minimum standards. But beyond that, effort can easily be wasted.

When I was studying for my marketing exams, part of the syllabus was the financial and numerical module. It's not that I can't do the math, it's just that I'm slow. Despite the extra tuition, progress was painful: whether it was statistics, discounted cash flow, reading a balance sheet, preparing a budget. The breakthrough came when I translated theory into practice. I found practical examples in my daily work to apply to every principle, and this meant that I was using the methods regularly.

Now, you'd never employ me as your FD, and it's much quicker to use an expert to crunch the numbers, but give me time, and I'll work back to first principles. What that means is that I share, or delegate, certain tasks to others. For example, for our Employee Engagement and other survey projects, I'll write the words and let our statistics expert prepare the numerical evidence. It's a strengths-based partnership.

What high-performance behavioral research tells us is that consistent behavior, especially when taken step by step toward the goal, is the key to success.

There's also the need to identify those for whom consistency is not a strength, especially if it's related to their main tasks. It's important to make links between business objectives and the consistent behaviors needed to achieve them. For salespeople, the links between contact management, lead generation, and making the call are vital to success. So consistent development of actions in these areas is going to be a must.

The underlying premise is that if you pay attention to the small details and consistently take care of them, you'll achieve the bigger goals. It makes sense. If you can apply a behavior consistently, you're more likely to achieve those bigger goals—especially goals based on peoples' strengths and behaviors with proven evidence of positive results. So, identifying and encouraging consistency is a way to both achieve greater success immediately and build a stronger, more resilient organization, populated with leaders at every level.

Three Ways to Identify and Encourage Consistency

Consistent behaviors with different types of people.

Flying back from Los Angeles one December, I traveled in a stretch limo with an international star of stage, screen, and soap operas, thanks to a mutual friend who'd introduced us. While I was in my comfortable "long haul" clothes, she was stunningly turned out from top to toe. I was looking for peace, quiet, and anonymity, while she was expecting to be recognized and photographed every step of the way.

Her attitude was simple: her audience is everywhere, and she owes it to them to live up to her billing. At each contact point, she was unfailingly polite, responding to autograph requests while queuing for the plane. What I noticed was that this behavior wasn't part of her act; it was an integral part of the warm person she is.

In the workplace, this means a consistent behavior with bosses, peers, and direct reports. This is a hugely engaging trait. People feel more at ease when they see that we're the same with them as with a senior person. The converse is also true: if we hear someone gossiping or dismissing someone else out of earshot, the chances are they'll behave in the same way when talking about us.

This kind of relationship consistency builds trust in the team (or reinforces distrust); it can build respect for line management and support for leaders—who tend to get lonely otherwise. Then there's the need for people to be consistent in their relationships with customers, suppliers, or joint venture partners. The financial implications to the customer base are obvious. And then there's consistency between people's workplace behaviors and how they are with family and friends. There are still those people who believe that family values and personal behaviors are irrelevant in the workplace. Yet that consistency, of applying high standards in the personal arena and transferring those behaviors into the domain of work, will reap rewards. These consistent relationship skills are vital in today's connected world.

Consistent Behaviors in Different, Even Volatile, Situations

Steamboat Springs, Colorado, on a clear day, is the most amazing place to be. From the hills above the town, you can see for miles in every direction. Unfortunately, we drove into town during one of the most powerful nighttime blizzards of the season. The station wagon was well equipped for most journeys, with winter tires and snow chains. The problem was that visibility dropped after we descended from Rabbit Ears Pass and the wind picked up.

Ending up in a ditch on the side of the road was really a "when, not if" scenario, despite every effort of the driver. I'd had my turn to drive earlier in the evening and was glad to hand it over. What was interesting, in hindsight, was how everyone responded so positively to the challenge of getting us out of the ditch and back on the road. We all got into our snow gear and piled out of the car to put our backs into the problem. Fortunately, we were rescued by the passing snow plough team, who cleared our path back to the road and set us on our way.

It was a couple of days later that we heard about "killing cold," where people lose their heads and make decisions that get them killed; that night, apparently, was one of them. One of the notable reasons for developing better leadership is to achieve consistency, even in volatile and changing situations. And when everyone buys into the notion of leadership where the whole team steps up and takes responsibility, the outcome is likely to be more positive.

This isn't the time for everyone to try and be "the leader," it's when people come together and collaborate as colleagues, for the common good. People who bring a stabilizing effect in uncertain times are valuable team members. Identifying and developing people with these personality traits will help in times of change. And this isn't the same as "bringing stability."

We can't make those promises anymore. Uncertainty is the new normal, and it's about rolling with the punches. Stability, in this context, is about how we behave toward one another to feel better about the uncertainty and the willingness to do what's necessary to tackle the challenges, as distinct from feeling ill-equipped and ill-prepared for change.

Volatility and uncertainty will affect most peoples' behavior, particularly when they feel under pressure. So, finding people who retain their usual standards, rather than fall apart or throw a tantrum because the external environment isn't to their liking, is essential.

People Who Are Patient in Competitive Environments

Especially when you want to encourage collaboration, such people are a great resource. Think of those points in the week when you need your normally competitive salespeople to come together and work on a shared goal. Or when things go horribly wrong: the team loses a contract or doesn't win the business they expected.

People who can consistently show empathy—and mean it—really support resilience in the team. This means that people will mourn together and bounce back more quickly than they otherwise would. It takes confidence to do something frequently and consistently. And when we're talking about positive and appropriate leadership and high-performance behaviors in times of volatility, having confident people in the workplace is a real bonus.

The behavior that needs more practice than most people imagine is the act of acknowledging someone. Acknowledgment isn't just about thanking people, although more of that would be nice. It is about noticing the underlying quality or values someone displays, through that act, because by seeing that, people are more likely to feel that you know and value them.

There's a belief in many managers that they strive to get the balance between acknowledgment and correction/development or performance issues about right. They believe that by balancing this in a 1:1 ratio (of acknowledgment to correction), they're doing okay as a boss. Sadly, this is not the perception of their teams. Typically, a manager has to increase the acknowledge-to-correct ratio by a factor of around five times for a member of their team to see them as being fair in their ratio.

So, not only are managers not getting the acknowledgment conversation right in the first place, they are also under-delivering on acknowledgments generally. And since acknowledgment of achievement, success, and behavior are key ways to motivate people and teams, it's an area in urgent need of improvement.

It's about frequency and repetition in applying leadership skills in our thinking, influencing, involving, and achieving behaviors. It's really not about theory—it is the practise of leadership, which requires practical leadership development. Part of the role of a leader is to see peoples' strengths and support them to use them more and more consistently. And this can happen at two levels: there are operational behaviors needed daily in the workplace, and there are those more strategic behaviors that will help take the organization forward in the future. Seeing peoples' strengths and identifying their potential is valuable for the individual, the team, and the organization.

Leadership development that supports consistency is key, and we'll look at this more in the next section. But developing people doesn't start in the leadership program; it starts with support from their line managers and colleagues. So that, rather than setting these people apart, they are supported to deliver daily in the workplace as well as grow into new and more challenging roles. We build consistent leadership behaviors one step at a time—starting with using that behavior with more people, applying them across different contexts, and then, using them more frequently. That's where the development phase starts. And the discovery phase is a vital step toward successful leadership development. Before we can successfully pick the best people to develop, we need to get past the central hero myth: the myth of the lone leader. It's about more than having a diversity mindset: it's seeing the value in every member of the team, not just those labeled "high achiever." Spotting team members' relationships skills and their ability to be consistent with people around them as they apply those skills is an important role for a line manager. Yet, even that task requires overcoming one's own leadership preferences and styles, acknowledging one's own unconscious biases and assumptions, and having a greater understanding of what the team and the organization needs to be successful in the VUCA World.

Worksheet: Stimulus Questions

In this chapter, we looked at the whole team—not just the stars—particularly through the lens of consistency in how they behave and what they deliver.

You can use this exercise for yourself and your own team or share it with colleagues to help them review their team in a new way.

What does your "vase" look like?

- Who are the big rocks?
- Who are the stones or pebbles?
- Who make up the gravel?
- What fills in the gaps, like sand?

What does "Consistency" Look Like in Your Team?

- Who's good at behaving in a consistently positive way?
- Who displays consistent behaviors in different, even volatile, situations and with different types of people?
- Who displays positive, motivating behaviors, like acknowledgments, frequently and consistently?

Overall, what does this tell you about your own leadership development needs or the development needs in your team?

Notes

1. J. Asplund, S. Agrawal, T. Hodges, J. Harter, and S. J. Lopez. 2007. March 2014. *The Clifton StrengthsFinder® 2.0 Technical Report: Development and Validation* (Washington, DC: Gallup Inc.).

CHAPTER 7

Soft Skills: Tougher Than They Look

Only one man in a thousand is a leader of men—the other 999 follow women.

—Groucho Marx

At some point in history, someone decided that core skills of communications, sociability, self-awareness, pretty much anything that tapped into our emotions, were a waste of money. To emphasize this point, they were labeled "soft skills" and were further downgraded as a result.

Soft, that is, until those same people discovered how vital these skills are to handling the so-called "difficult" conversations—conversations with people different to themselves, about performance, better teamwork, and improving delivery.

Until, that is, professional services, like doctors, dentists, and other health professionals, discovered that poor communications are linked to:

- Being struck off from professional practice
- Poor compliance with medical regimens
- Overtreating and overmedicating
- Ignoring the patient's voice and symptoms
- High "did not attend" appointment rates

As you'd expect, there's a price tag on this cost[1]:

- "... a survey of 400 companies with 100,000 employees each cited an average loss per company of $62.4 million per year" (David Grossman)

- " . . . miscommunication cost even smaller companies of 100 employees an average of $420,000 per year" (Debra Hamilton)

These types of conversation are perceived as "difficult" because they require strong emotional intelligence (EQ).

They're "difficult" because in avoiding the root cause of the issues, people make out the issues to be more "complex" than they are, creating a mist of confusion to avoid confronting underlying issues.

At the same time, employers create environments that put people under huge pressure yet expect "resilient" behaviors, where they miraculously bounce back in the face of adversity.

In today's increasingly complex world, core communications skills, alongside this sociability, are vital. Coaching and mentoring skills are emerging as systematic ways to bring the best out of people and teams. Key elements both in leadership development, and key skills for leaders and managers themselves. Or, as Derek Bok once said: *"If you think education is expensive, try ignorance."*

In this chapter we'll look at why these skills are vital to develop, particularly in leaders and managers, and why they are the best place to start in the development process.

Prevention Really is Better than Cure

Our research findings puzzled us.

We'd been asked by a client to evaluate two development programs against some key behaviors, including managing conflict.

On every other measure, one program stood out.

Leaders and managers were actively supporting staff to discover solutions for themselves, by asking open questions and employing open and flexible communication styles with their staff. Elements were independently identified as creating a group of motivated leaders using a sustainable process.

What this group **weren't** doing was reporting that they were managing conflict; whereas the second group were.

This matters because conflict costs time, money, and energy. It drains motivation from people, creating "heart sink" moments for leaders and managers. Many people believe that the best way to improve the situation is to learn how to "manage" difficult people; "man up" and have those "difficult" conversations.

Not satisfied with the research results, we dug a little deeper and ran some interviews among the two groups. What we found both surprised and delighted us.

They weren't managing conflict, because conflict wasn't arising.

Yes, they still disagreed, but here was a group of leaders working to prevent honest debate turning into heated conflict.

We asked them what they did instead and found that their responses aligned closely to better leadership behavior models:

- They encouraged staff to explore alternative ideas and solutions
- They actively listened to staff concerns, goals, values, and beliefs
- They provided clear and direct feedback

And, most importantly of all, they acknowledged what people had achieved; so the conversations were based on the staff's strengths, skills, and experience they brought to the table.

Team members' questioning and exploring behavior wasn't labeled "challenging"; rather, it was received as a valuable contribution to the debate.

This means that managers' energy, time, and effort were freed up to get on with the task of delivering.

Communication Skills Development

Those "soft" skills are tougher than they look.

It meant that leaders didn't feel the need to invest energy in defending their positions or decisions; rather, they took input as part of a shared ongoing learning experience.

This is a more mature response to a potentially ego-threatening conversation.

Of course, because the leaders had ultimate responsibility for certain decisions, it meant that their staff didn't always agree with them.

Our respondents told us that this became part of the ongoing honest conversations, which included demonstrating the rationale for a decision in a transparent fashion, rather than a "because I say so" rebuttal.

This communications style can be summed up as "coachlike leadership."

It is termed "coachlike" because the professional executive coach has a more independent, objective perspective and takes a partnership role in the conversation.

A leader–team-member conversation is always going to be one of unequal power, where both parties are subject to shared goals, objectives, and deadlines.

Both leader and team member are working within a framework, but deploying coaching skills can create win–win relationships.

The "coachlike" leader can also achieve better performance, reach higher sales targets, and maintain better working relationships with team members by using those techniques.

Coachlike leaders have the skills to separate out the attitude and intention from the behavior, such that expectations of the team are focused on effective behaviors yet appreciate people's good intentions and their desire to succeed.

Using these skills is a pragmatic conflict prevention and reduction strategy.

Emotional Intelligence Skills Development

Yet sometimes it's impossible to avoid conflict, born as it is out of pressure, stressful situations, and life beyond the control of even the best leader or manager.

This is where emotional intelligence development and resilience training comes in. For many people and organizations, "resilience" is just about the person, the individual's abilities to "bounce back" from challenge and change.

This ability to recover from challenge is not a constant. We all have factors in our life that knock us for six, either in the present or from our past.

Giving ourselves ways—as well as time—to recover from setbacks is critical to resilience. And sometimes it takes a leader to support others to even give themselves time and permission to "recover."

The common term for this is "bounce back," yet this implies a quick return to the norm. It can take a while to recover from some of the knocks life throws at us. And when those knocks come one after the other, there is a cumulative effect that can't be ignored.

Resilience works hand in hand with workload management, and this leads us back to the point that organizational factors, the work environment, the systems and individual factors are all important.

At the organizational level, the resources the organization puts in place to support positive change will reduce personal and team conflict, and this starts with building better leadership.

Managers and leaders have a responsibility to develop their own emotional intelligence skills and to evoke them in others: teams and individuals alike.

There are a number of dimensions of emotional intelligence, and every one of them is developable:

- Self-awareness
- Emotional resilience
- Motivation
- Interpersonal sensitivity
- Influence
- Intuitiveness
- Conscientiousness

Leaders can support this development by really getting to know their people—their strengths and development areas, what already motivates them, and how to build that motivation.

Daniel Goleman summarizes these skills into four areas of inner attitudes and external behaviors: self-awareness, self-management, social awareness, and relationship management.

A great example of using EQ skills in the area of relationship management came with a coaching client who worked with his team to come up with some creative time and money saving ideas.

One of these included influencing two competing suppliers to share a single workspace so that the resources they offered were more readily available to the customer in a rural location.

There was no financial or other downside to either supplier, other than the move.

The key challenge was that of being willing to work more collaboratively. Using his EQ skills of motivation, interpersonal sensitivity, and influence, the leader enabled both parties to see the win–win and share in the savings.

Leaders can also help to organize the workload such that it plays to people's strengths—and doesn't overwhelm people.

It's a key difference between a leader and a manager.

- A well-managed workload—such that people get the job done within a reasonable time span—is about task management.
- Leadership is about tapping into people's motivation such that they meet those task deadlines.

Task success is also about individuals' conscientiousness to get the job done well, the self-awareness to know one's own strengths and development areas.

These are all so-called "soft skills" that can be harnessed to deliver more for the organization.

Leaders also need to understand what "empowerment" really means and put ways in place to deliver. Again, this taps into skills such as delegation, which in turn requires qualities such as evoking trust and respect in team members.

High-Performance Behavior Development

Practical issues need to be taken care of, such as managing expectations, identifying clear delivery paths or ways of working.

These are all high-performance behaviors that are part of a group of twelve skills vital to any leadership development program.

For example, good leadership requires that a culture of learning is embedded in the team for the benefit of everyone. Only when everyone is a "hero," contributing to that learning in an inclusive way, facilitated by the leader, can true organizational learning evolve. This is a developable leadership behavior.

There are, to be sure, some organizations that involve particularly demanding circumstances: military, health, and other "blue light" emergency services, such as police or fire professionals, are some examples.

Doctors and soldiers alike describe the tactics they employ to switch off their emotions, in tune with the professionalism that is called for to get the job done through traumatic times.

It's the role of the leader to ensure that these people's workloads are such that these challenges don't overwhelm them, however much the circumstances may seem that way.

This isn't about patting someone on the back and sympathizing; it's about recovery time after particularly challenging situations.

It's also the role of the organization, or institution, to support people to relearn and reconnect with their emotional strengths, such that they can "switch back" into everyday society and its norms.

It's one thing to learn how to switch off from the emotional triggers that most people are affected by, but the ability to discriminate between triggers and to re-engage emotionally, appropriately, is a key challenge.

Examples of this can be found in the military and police forces around the world. People are trained to move forward, quickly, in times of trouble. Not to think but to engage, to get into action. This is great in conflict zones, but not in social situations, and certainly not when ordinarily decent people misread the signals and escalate to conflict when de-escalation is the better solution.

Soft Skills: The Success Link between Leaders and Teams

Teams need EQ too, as the work of Dulewicz and Higgs[2] makes clear. Not every team needs the same culture, but they do need to be able to work together on problems, not as a "group of individuals" or pitted, competitively, against another department.

It's important for the team to own their challenges together. To address change, introduce improvements; try them out and celebrate success. It also means that the team can push back when overloaded; finding ways for that "well-managed workload" to become a reality by using their influencing and negotiating skills.

This means that team members need to find constructive ways to give and receive feedback and, most importantly, to own "failure" and find ways back from that.

A coaching or mentoring conversation is an adult-to-adult conversation. More than a transactional "if you do this, then. . . ." dialogue, it's a transformational conversation where the leader embodies good leadership, as a role model for the team.

The individual factors in developing soft skills include knowing one's own boundaries, such that we can develop resilience, together with the other EQ skills.

Knowing the theory isn't enough; having a wider range of language for emotions (and we're not talking four-letter words here) and knowing which triggers are most likely to affect our emotions—positively or negatively—really helps.

Consciously practicing the EQ skills is also important, whether that's by asking others for feedback on a particular skill or taking one and using it in different situations.

Ways to Develop Leadership Skills

Too many leadership development programs are based around analyzing and fixing weaknesses. Too much training money is invested here.

Assuming people have more than the basic abstract, verbal, and numerical reasoning skills, plus the ability to read a financial report and manage a budget, the best place to invest in skill development is in building upon people's strengths.

The rationale for this is that it provides a confidence boost and a track record on which to then address other development areas.

Starting with development needs means starting from a low emotional base, where defensiveness ("why do I need to change?") and other negative reactions can act as a developmental barrier.

Leadership development also typically starts with external behaviors, even when it's shifts like attitude change that they're trying to create.

I find it fascinating that people accept this point in theory, yet push back strongly when it comes to reality. So many learning and development designers, and leaders and managers, strongly feel the need to push people "out of their comfort zones." For some reason the "discomfort zone as a good thing" paradigm prevails.

Now, don't get me wrong; I'm not saying we don't all need to stretch and grow. The difference is, who's dictating the challenge?

When leadership development starts from inner strengths rather than outer skills, it's easier to embed new behaviors.

When people take on a challenge, rather than being thrown into it, you'll have higher intrinsic motivation.

And there's a good psychological reason to encourage intrinsic motivation: Put simply, we're more likely to stick it out when times get tough.

My recent challenge was to take 2 weeks improving my Italian, in Italy. Working closely with our business partners showed me how poor my language skills were. So I took myself off to Trieste for some intense learning.

The early morning of day 1 was particularly tough. It was dark, cold, and wet, and I was on my way to a 30-minute exam. I remember asking myself what on earth I was doing this for.

By day 3, I had reached rock bottom. Tired from the focus; trying to understand my tutor (no mobile phones or dictionaries allowed; we only spoke Italian). And it felt like I was making no progress.

Then something shifted. I understood, really "in the moment" understood, what someone said to me. It felt like a switch had been turned on in my brain and there was light.

The progress I made after that point was much faster. I was able to tap into all the vocabulary I had in store, and conversations flowed. (Well, they didn't stagger along as they had previously.)

If new behaviors can be summarized as being "ready, willing, and able" to perform a task, then readiness and willingness need to be developed first.

That's because when willingness and readiness to change are already taken care of: it's just the skills and abilities associated with the task that need to be addressed.

Of course, systematic course design matters.

But if people don't feel ready or willing to change, then the learned behaviors won't embed. By starting a leadership development program with all these elements, the whole program will be more successful.

Peer Learning Methods

When we worked with a national rail organization as part of a leadership development program for more than 2,000 people, the pilot phase put the leadership coaching skills workshop in the middle.

At the 12-month review stage, it was clear that the participants valued this workshop highly, because it not only helped them to work with their teams in practical ways to improve performance, but also helped the learners gel together as a team.

So being a willing learner, surrounded and supported by other willing learners, also matters.

In the "rollout" phase, the coaching skills workshop was moved to the beginning of the program, which embedded the values of a leadership and learning culture, combined with practical coaching skills, into the whole program.

Of course, it's not enough just to value a learning opportunity. It's vital to put those skills into practice as early as possible, because that is the only way we can we build up our competence in them.

And it's only by seeing the benefit of those applied skills that we see the return on the significant investments in employee learning and development.

This means that skills application must be supported, not just taught. This is the value of combining classroom learning with on-the-job support, preferably soon after the initial learning.

Peer learning includes peer coaching, and, in some circumstances, mentoring. So learning these skill sets in a leadership development program is a practical step.

Facilitated peer learning is particularly valuable in this regard. We call them PALS—Peer Action Learning Sets—by which we mean having a tutor facilitate conversations between course participants on how they are applying their learning; what they've learned about what does and doesn't work.

The tutor focuses on the leadership behaviors (identified at the "define" stage as important to the organization) and on supporting participants to see how these are being applied.

It's more than just facilitating a conversation; it's helping learners to identify what works and to shift their behaviors toward consistent application of successful behaviors.

The goal is to train learners in the PALS method and ease out the tutor so that once the participants are familiar with the high-performance behaviors expected of them, they facilitate their own learning sets.

Measure the Impacts

Identifying and measuring impacts is a key challenge in the field of leadership development.

Knowing what and how to measure impact is context specific, and therefore return on investment (ROI) should be closely linked to the aims and objectives of the learning; specifically, to the reported outcomes linked to the learning and the observed leadership behaviors of participants back in the workplace.

For one (financial services) client, we measured the impacts of a Manager as Coach soft skills workshop using before and after surveys in three factors: feeling confidence, being equipped to deliver, being effective in coaching conversations. Most people reported double-digit improvements afterwards, except for one group who either remained the same or dropped their scores. This group reported themselves as having over rated themselves first time around. Known as the Dunning-Kruger effect, this is where people over estimate their abilities, and which can be linked to blind spots as to their competence. 360 degree feedback methods can help provide more objective evidence in these situations, for everyone's benefit.

Using these tough "soft skills" delivers real value to the organization.

If ever a myth needed to be nailed, it's the myth that skills like empathy; relationship management; better communications between leaders and peers, customers, or patients are "soft."

These skills are vital to our success in every area of relationships: as leaders, in teams, and as individual human beings.

Soft skills are tougher than they first appear. They have a vital role in the workplace.

These skills may not be visible to the organization, in terms of physical outputs, but their value can be measured in costs avoided, conflict reduced, and innovation increased.

The biggest challenge is that we take these skills for granted and only value them when they've gone. As the song says, "You don't know what you've got till it's gone." And when conflict reappears and performance drops, it's a lesson to be learned all over again.

Worksheet: Stimulus Questions

In this chapter we looked at the value of so-called "soft skills." You might care to do a financial audit on the costs to your organization of poor communications, but an easier way might be to identify key areas where improved communications could benefit individuals and teams.

We focus, in this chapter, on the skills of communication, coaching, emotional intelligence, and peer learning.

For this piece of fieldwork, we encourage you to undertake a survey and ask your colleagues, leaders, and managers these questions:

- What benefits do they see in having and deploying these skills (listed below)?
- Who is most likely to benefit as a result of improvements in these areas?
- What's likely to be different as a result?
- What time, money, L&D, or other investment costs might be needed?

Skills Checklist

- Better communications
- Successful (annual/quarterly, etc.) performance reviews
- Difficult conversations
- Conflict Prevention
- Improved Emotional intelligence
- Coaching skills for managers and leaders

- High-performance behavior development
- Shifting learning from weakness to strengths-thinking
- Facilitated Peer Learning

Notes

1. P.M. Buhler and J.D. Worden. 2013. "Up, Down, and Sideways: High-Impact Verbal Communication for HR Professionals (SHRM)," quoting *The Cost of Poor Communications* SHRM.org, https://www .shrm.org/resourcesandtools/hr-topics/behavioral-competencies/ communication/pages/the-cost-of-poor-communications.aspx, (accessed March 17, 2018). quoting David Grossman D., (author of *The Cost of Poor Communications*) and Hamilton D.
2. V. Dulewicz and M. Higgs. 2000. "Emotional intelligence— A review and evaluation study." *Journal of Managerial Psychology* 15, no. 4, pp. 341–72.

CHAPTER 8

Leadership by Lion Taming

For ten years Caesar ruled with an iron hand. Then with a wooden foot, and finally with a piece of string.

—Spike Milligan

One of our most experienced colleagues and mentors told us:

When customers look at developing their people what they see on offer is either evidence-based learning, or "leadership by lion taming." The risk is they get seduced by the glamour; they buy with their heart, not their head.

Allied to the current myth that hero leadership is the best model for organizations is the belief that the best development investment is to create leaders who feel like heroes.

Whether it's taking one for the team by swimming across a lake, abseiling, or white water rafting, action leadership development is a popular choice.

Yet these activities waste money, time, and effort.

Of course, they're great fun. No question.

The issue is, what observable leadership behaviors do they instill, support, and encourage?

Then there are the "sheep dip" development activities, where people are trained, in robot fashion, to supervise their team members through the carrot and the stick.

Some people say there's no evidence for the success of these methods. We argue that there's plenty: that these superficial approaches have the opposite effect to that intended.

When we invest in fads, such as leadership by lion taming, flying a jet, or driving a fast car around a track, we send clear messages to the people being led that their regular contribution doesn't matter—it's all about rewarding the hero. And if you climb the career ladder (preferably without a safety net and the ropes on fire), you can be a hero too.

Now, don't get us wrong. If your organization is looking to become the next "Cirque de Soleil," we can see the value of this approach.

Or if the purpose is to attract attention for a charity and do something totally daring and out of your comfort zone, we're wholeheartedly behind you.

Why? Because you've chosen that challenge for yourself. You're willing to put up with the pain of training and the fear of failure to benefit a cause dear to you and your family's heart. We salute you. You're an inspiration. We wholeheartedly support your efforts. This is heroism.

But is it leadership?

In this chapter we explore the importance of having a clear vision for leadership development, knowing the behaviors you want to promote in leaders and team members alike.

We look at the paradox of developing the inner person, contrasted with measuring the observable behaviors. The difference between pushing someone out of their "comfort zone" and tapping into their inner drive to stretch and challenge themselves.

We explore the iceberg model of development and the self-consistency theory, both of which can be used to harness personal development and change.

A client was asking for help, but could we discuss it outside the office? She warned that if anyone overheard the conversation, she'd be labeled as ungrateful and out of step with the organization.

The problem? Her top team had recently been sent on a "leadership" course run by a fire and rescue organization. The cost, a high one, had come out of her budget and, far from seeing the promised benefits, a macho culture was now running rampant in a previously collaborative team.

Motivated by activities involving climbing ladders, brandishing hoses, and races involving dismantling and reassembling equipment, the team returned expecting a higher level of energy and activity back in the workplace.

The good news was that they were very familiar with which extinguisher to use in which fire situation.

Otherwise, the benefits were far from clear.

The impact of this fell on front-line staff, who were given extra tasks such as reorganizing the stores and polishing obsolete equipment, much in the manner of the Home Guard expecting an inspection from Captain Mainwaring (a character from a UK BBC comedy program).

And again, don't mistake me. Having a tidy store, knowing where to get your hands on the right equipment quickly, is important.

But this was above and beyond what was needed. The normal routines of her maintenance unit were set aside in pursuit of the unusual and heroic. Small errors crept in; tasks were left undone and complaints rose.

The crisis came when a health and safety incident nearly escalated out of proportion. Fortunately, the incident was minor, but the implications had shocked the senior team.

After debriefing the immediate incident and supporting the client to cover all the bases, we turned our attention to the underlying issues: What leadership behaviors do you need your direct reports to display?

Which of these do they already have? Which do you need to develop?

Leadership Essentials: Purpose

Having a big picture purpose statement for anything is essential. It creates a guiding star toward which to aim. And, like painting by numbers, you fill in the gaps and evaluate the skills and talents you already have to meet the need. It's also a baseline against which to measure progress.

And there's a difference between a vision and a goal. A vision is a picture of how life will be like in the new future, what success looks and feels like. It's a clear image that will tell people they've got there.

Leadership purpose statements are defined by how people will feel to be part of the team in this new era; how running the department will look; what people will say about the team that's different from today; what's important to the team; what resources are available in this environment; what the challenges are, and how the leadership will help the team meet those challenges.

Goals are the action steps toward the vision. But unless you know where you are going, what's important about that vision and direction and what's expected of leaders in this environment, any actions will be directionless and uncontrolled.

Some people, including our client, like to set out the problems clearly too, just so that they know—and can be reminded—why they set off on this path.

Leadership Essentials: High-performance Behaviors

One in-depth area to explore is the leadership purpose. What behaviors are expected of people in this environment, such that others can see everyone working toward the same purpose?

These fall into four clusters:

1. Behaviors that support and encourage a greater breadth and depth of exploration and thinking
2. Leadership behaviors that develop and motivate others by finding out about them as people
3. Leadership that demonstrates the direction and purpose of the organization, department, or team, through building confidence, having impact and presenting well.
4. The achieving behaviors: being proactive, measuring progress, making improvements as you go, and having a success mindset.

Each team, department, or organization will need its own blend with an emphasis on one behavior cluster or another.

Typical of many back office teams, a logistics customer had a learning and development team that delivered well yet lacked visibility in the organization.

People on the front line were regularly sent on courses; they rated them highly but gave them no more thought once their busy day jobs took over.

Research identified this lack of visibility with the relatively low application of skills back in the workplace. And, given the shift to a range of online learning tools being developed, the client needed the workforce to be more aware of, and to value, their learning opportunities.

The irony was that this was a team of trainers who were great at delivering but less great at promoting their skills and successes. It's a classic behavior trait of delivering the work, but not celebrating the quality, success, or impacts.

Since customer focus was a strategic objective for the whole organization, it was clear that this ran like a seam of gold ready to be mined.

Once the training delivery team created their purpose statement for what success looked and felt like, it became clear that the clusters to develop were in the areas of demonstrating impact and building confidence in others about the impact that great training had on the wider organization.

They also linked those behavior needs to the achievement cluster, because they realized that once a program was delivered, they quickly moved on to the next, rather than finding ways to prove, demonstrate, and share the impacts.

As expert workshop designers, they developed a program that both aligned with the organization's bigger purpose picture and stood out enough to have the desired impact.

It also helped them develop their work in demonstrating the impacts of what they delivered to the business: people who attended their customer service training achieved meaningful results in terms of new business achieved, customers retained, and business expansion.

Leadership Essentials: Evidence

No one likes to see money wasted on ineffective training programs, and the simple addition of an impact assessment helps identify those wasted efforts and those that are having a significant impact.

Evidence is simply that: evidence.

However, it raises fears and concerns that dark secrets will be uncovered; hard truths need to be faced. An oft-repeated maxim about marketing is that half of it is wasted, but the trick is knowing which half.

The good news is that in today's digital world we can benchmark and measure progress quickly, easily, and affordably.

So now you can look at the people who go through your development programs and see which method corresponds to their preferred learning style and suits them best. You can do the following:

- Measure which topics people find easiest to relate to and which the hardest.

- Measure the pace of in-person or live online learning events and adjust accordingly.
- Test the average time to complete self-paced learning programs.

There's simply no need to have "one size fits all" or "sheep dip" development programs anymore. It's a simple matter to help personalize people's learning, even within the wider framework of overall development aims and objectives.

Clients regularly ask us to create "personal development plans" (or PDPs) tailored to their organization's high-performance competences and values. Different professions, such as the UK "GDC" or General Dental Council, also expect professionals to keep a PDP.

Notice the Less-visible Leadership Behaviors

Having a tailored PDP is as valuable for your one-to-one coaching programs as your team and group development.

It's great for all types of leadership behaviors, especially for the less visible and underdeveloped behaviors such as the thinking clusters.

These internal "behaviors" are harder for traditional training programs to develop and measure. They often remain undervalued, with lip service paid to them.

We often ask people if they use the "plan, do, review" cycle in their project leadership, and most often the answer is "yes." And then we ask how much time, exactly, they spend in each of these areas?

Typically, the "review" step gets the least time.

And what does a "review" meeting look like? Is it a "what went wrong, who's to blame?" discussion, by any chance?

The thinking cluster of leadership behaviors are given so little time or priority, it's no wonder that innovation and creativity are stifled.

We give time to things we value, and, typically, we value things we can see. Unless we go looking for specific behaviors, we can't see the thinking, review, and reflection that's a vital part of a learning organization.

In addition to the typical review meeting, there's the practice of having a team write a review. That's great for the authors, but unless that review gets widely shared and communicated it's of little value elsewhere.

A review process where people invest time in reflecting on what worked, what might be done differently going forward, what really had an impact—and what didn't—is of far more value than a report gathering dust on a shelf or tucked away in a digital cloud file storage system.

Use Coaching to Develop Leadership Behaviors

This is where one-to-one and team or group coaching come in—because professional coaches are taught how to ask those truly thought-provoking, powerful questions that move people to a deeper level of leadership behaviors:

- More flexible thinking
- Deeper, and wider, information search
- Digging for more options, not just the superficial or first ideas
- Making connections, joining up the dots between ideas, so that true innovation can happen

Developing the inner person isn't a vanity project. It's probably the most untapped resource you have in your organization.

If all your people do every day is the "doing" but no learning, creativity, or innovation is happening, then you're going to be stuck where you are today, rather than moving forward to achieve your purpose.

When we value something we give it time. We throw money at it.

Developing the inner person isn't yet one of those things. There's plenty of global interest in personal, inner development: as the multibillion mindfulness and meditation movements remind us.

The Iceberg Model

The image that explains its importance, to most people, is the iceberg model, where 90 percent of our thoughts, beliefs, values, and emotions lie untapped and hidden under the surface.

In the past these emotions were feared, and even rejected in the workplace. People were asked not to bring their emotions into work.

Times have changed. In the global thought economy, we need people to have the energy and passion to sustain their motivation.

We now know that emotional engagement with the organization by employees will improve safety, efficiency, productivity, and profits.

Tapping into the inner person becomes essential.

The classic method comes from the days of "command and control" leadership: get people out of their comfort zones. Put them into uncomfortable situations and then expect them to behave differently as a result.

Most Western leadership development comes out of North American military training, so it's not surprising that these were the methods used.

After all, your organization is just like a military operation, isn't it? (Answer: probably not!)

Ex-military people thrive in transport and logistics environments where routine and attention to this kind of detail is vital. Or where crises are inevitable. Bluelight services, especially ambulance transportation, traditionally benefit from this kind of thinking.

Unsurprisingly, it's less than effective in sectors where creativity and innovation need to flourish. Relaxation and comfort create environments where these ideas can be seeded and thrive.

And that might be an ambulance service or a distribution center run by robots.

One of our clients was challenged to transform a network of ambulance services. They used to be run in the traditional manner: van-sized vehicles operating from a city center location close to the control office.

Then someone said: "Why don't we have our teams located closer to the likely accident hot spots, like the motorway?"

And someone else said: "and why don't we have smaller vehicles for the city centre?"

And then someone said: "and how about using bicycles or tricycles?"

And someone else said: "and why don't we take the A&E specialist to the emergency callout, instead of transporting the patient to A&E?"

Not all of these ideas were taken up by the particular regional service, but all these ideas are in operation somewhere in the UK.

Once again, context is everything. And why environment matters.

If you want to have focused, decisive meetings where targets are met and people get into action, holding those meetings in a low-ceilinged room will help. The focus is narrow and on what's right in front of the team. Comfort doesn't matter because you're not going to be there long.

For broader thinking, creativity, and innovation, high ceilings and more light will help. Distractions and off-topic elements help seed new ideas and new ways of thinking. Comfort does matter, because the brain will leap around in new ways in low-pressure environments.

Once again, the development environment depends on what you're trying to achieve. The delivery environment matters too, and both need to be aligned. More of that in part four.

The Self-consistency Model

One final element in the development phase is a reminder that your leadership development goals can be aligned with people's own inner values.

People like to know that what they're being asked to do, or develop, is consistent with their inner map of themselves.

Helping them make links between their own values and the values and purpose behind their development will speed up commitment and motivation needed to succeed in the development program.

Self-consistency theory means that we can do away with the "leadership by lion taming" fads that exist to stimulate and excite people.

You can save the thrills and spills for the celebrations, rather than the development days.

People get more lasting fulfillment and satisfaction from seeing the difference made by a meaningful and personalized program, and from seeing the impact it has back in the workplace, than from short-term sensory stimulation.

We see this regularly in the difference between the open leadership development programs we run and our corporate client work.

If you've been "sent" on a program, no matter how well meaning the sponsor was or how beneficial this might be to your future career, you're going to be less committed to it than someone who sees how it's consistent with their own values.

If attendance is a "reward" for past performance, there's no guarantee that it will motivate people in the future—until the next reward carrot is dangled. This approach may work for some work cultures, such as sales, where competition and rewards feature highly, but it's not a great basis for sustainable leadership.

Worse is when people assume that they're being sent on a program to fix some kind of problem, when maybe someone has seen their potential and believes they're doing them a service by putting them forward for development.

In contrast, people who have greater control over the development choice, or have worked with their line manager or human resources (HR) partner to shape their development path, show greater commitment to the efforts required to complete a leadership development program.

This is where those personal development plans, and step two, Discover, come in.

Having a discovery conversation that creates win-win in terms of leadership development is a valuable investment.

We're not talking about spoon-feeding people here, or about setting up false expectations of promotion or other advancement, but rather, a conversation that helps people see how a leadership development program that they get to shape is an investment in their personal and professional development, not just a benefit to the organization.

Development Impacts the Whole Team

This is a conversation that needs to include line managers too. When adjustments need to be made to accommodate the learning commitment, it's not fair to expect line managers and team colleagues to take up that slack without any support.

Having a clear sense of the future benefits of developing people and demonstrating support to the rest of the team during the development period is an integral part of the development program.

One client recently mentioned how undervalued she felt when she saw her colleagues getting up to go to the next management training session, while she was left to answer the phones and pick up the slack.

This is probably how you'd feel if it happened to you.

So the messages we send out all matter, whether they're to managers, course participants, and the colleagues left to cover while participants are out.

Clarity about the messages you want to get across is vital for the wider success of the project and its intended long-term, positive, impacts.

When we're asking people to give up their time—either leisure time or worktime that could be usefully spent getting the day job delivered—we need to be sure that the motivation is there.

When it is, the lengths to which people go to work together, complete their assignments, or learn new ideas is simply inspirational.

Leadership development is a huge investment. And it is one that must pay reasonable returns. By putting in the preparation to define the leadership needs and decide who are the best people to invest in, waste can be significantly reduced.

Additionally, by investing in the most untapped area of talent—people's inner values, beliefs, and motivation—we can release huge potential, aligned with both the organization's needs and people's sense of themselves.

Modern technologies also give us the opportunity to personalize learning to a degree unachievable before. We don't need to put people through such things as "standard programs," and we can use coaching and mentoring support to further personalize the learning and develop people's innate and individual potential even further.

The return on investment of this kind of development is both measurable and traceable. You'll know where you're getting the best returns and where to cut back and where to invest further to get the development results your leaders, teams, and your organization need.

Worksheet: Stimulus Questions

In this chapter we looked at the need for leadership development to be led not only by the needs of the organization, but also by the behaviors the organization is looking for—not by the fads and high-octane activities that we define as "leadership by lion taming"

In this reflective exercise, we think about not only the leadership behaviors you're looking for as an organization, but also the messages you want to send out about leadership development.

Message Clarity

What are the top three messages you need to convey to the whole organization about your leadership development strategy?

Given the answers to 1, what style of leadership development do you need?

- Adventure/outward bound
- Interactive/engaging/game-focused
- Interactive/intellectual
- Interactive/emotionally driven
- Lecture/theory
- A mix of the above

Or something else?

Your Learning Blend

What's the mix of learning methods that you need?

- In-person
- Live, distance learning—by video, audio, conference call
- Self-paced learning (e.g., ELearning)
- 1-1 coaching/mentoring
- Group coaching/mentoring
- PALS (Peer Action Learning Sets)

Use percentages to define what the mix might look like—e.g., 60 percent self-paced; 20 percent live, distance learning; 10 percent 1-1 PALS 10 percent 1-1 coaching, and consider your rationale for this blend.

CHAPTER 9

Well, Nobody's Perfect

The man who smiles when things go wrong has thought of someone to blame it on.

—Robert Bloch

The show *Who Wants to Be a Millionaire?* is a huge success, shown in around 160 countries.

The show did have an issue in one country, however, at the point when contestants ask the audience for their advice. What normally happens is that the audience genuinely give the best answer they can. However, in this one country, the audience tends to deliberately mislead the contestants by voting for the wrong answer. It's a cultural attitude toward another's success—or failure.

Leadership is a daily practice, a journey, not a destination. We believe that journeys should be as fulfilling—or even as enjoyable—as the destination. That means we practice, and sometimes fail, to be good leaders. Sometimes, it's not the thing we fail at that's the problem, but our attitude toward failure itself.

In leadership development, we often use our leadership 360 survey ("my360plus") to gather feedback around the capability or competence model that the organization uses.

The purpose of this is to support the individual in developing their leadership capacity.

Raters don't all behave in the same way as the game show audience; however, the degree to which they will be objective varies depending on their own motivation, the quality of the questions in the 360, and the capability model itself.

I worked in one organization where they linked the results of the 360 to pay.

It went one of two ways: you got together with your colleagues to create a pact whereby everybody rated everybody well; some of the more competitive individuals went off and ranked everybody else as low as they could, in the belief that this would enhance their own chances of a good pay raise.

The "link to pay" idea quickly feel by the wayside.

Leadership Essentials: 360° Feedback

We ran a leadership development programme for an international organization in four countries across three continents.

One of the key elements was a 360 survey. There were around a hundred people in the program, and we always expected there to be some variation across that group. Inevitably, when selecting a talent pool of that size, there will be differences in their abilities.

What we hadn't factored in were the cultural differences that led people to rate their colleagues in different ways.

Several individuals were rated at the highest possible level in every single one of the twelve competences. This may have felt good for the rater, but it was hard for the individual to select an area to work on.

I'm not arguing that a 360 has no value; when it is well designed, well briefed, combined with other sources, and debriefed effectively by the boss or a coach, it has huge value.

It's about our expectations of people, set against whatever leadership model your organization uses.

In the preceding examples, the results will be skewed toward greatness or indifference because of the biases and subjectivity that people might be tempted to bring in.

Leadership Essentials: Neutralize Limitations

But even when ratings are done with the best intentions, with a desire to support the individual to improve, there are often inherent flaws in our expectations of the process and the people.

Most performance management systems have an implicit expectation that we should be excellent everywhere, and that the way to achieve this is to focus on, and improve, our weaknesses.

This approach is fundamentally flawed.

Not only is it impossible to be good at everything; it's also untrue to assume there is only one approach to successful leadership.

Look at the diversity of approaches that different leaders take. No one would say that Winston Churchill and Gandhi shared the same style, but, equally, no one could contest the huge successes that each brought in their own way.

Our first instinct, though, when we see any form of appraisal is still to go look for the weaknesses. We are drawn there like a moth to the flame, with predictably painful outcomes.

If we are the recipient of this feedback, we might start to argue with it, to justify ourselves against this benchmark.

If we are the manager giving the feedback, the danger is that we see this person in front of us as being flawed, because she hasn't impressed in every competence. It impacts on our overall view of performance in a negative way.

One organization that we work with had, until recently, dozens of competences explained in a guide of around 120 pages. It would be crazy to assume that anybody could be good at all of them.

And if it takes a 120-page manual to explain the behaviors, the chances of them being applied in any consistent or meaningful way is slight.

The same is true even when your organization uses only eight or 12 or 16 competences.

Nobody is going to be good at everything, and the danger is we often waste time trying to "fix" the weaknesses when the same level of investment building their strengths would have a far higher return on investment.

You grow most in your areas of greatest strength. You will improve the most, be the most creative, be the most inquisitive, and bounce back the fastest in those areas where you have already shown some natural advantage over everyone else—your strengths. This doesn't mean you should ignore your weaknesses. It just means you'll grow most where you're already strong.

Marcus Buckingham[1]

That's not to say that limitations, or "derailers" as they're sometimes known, shouldn't be addressed. If a behavior is having a negative impact on others, then it's a priority. Likewise, if a behavior is negatively impacting a leader's ability to deliver on their role, it's a priority.

Leadership Essentials: Develop Strengths

I was recently in Zambia, running a development centre. We had a day off and visited the Chaminuka game reserve. The highlight for me was the chance to interact with two 6-month-old cheetah cubs.

I had no idea how kindly they would feel toward humans and began to run through my list of strengths to see if any would be of use to me.

The team were trying to reintroduce cheetahs to the wild. At the same time, they are using the cubs as part of an education program.

They take them to schools, to inspire the next generation to value these endangered species. The worst predators for cheetahs are, unsurprisingly, men. It was clear the handlers loved their job, had a passion for nature, and reveled in showing us humans how to respect these elegant creatures.

When working with leaders, we use the Clifton Strengthsfinder,[2] a great tool for assessing key talents and strengths. It's based on research around how our brains evolve in the first 13 or so years of our life.

Pathways determined by our genes are strengthened through our experience and lead us to build talents. For example, some people acquire a thirst for learning; others may be driven to maximize their efforts in any walk of life.

Or you may love working one to one with people or be a great communicator. All these traits start early in life. Understanding them is key to finding the role that really suits you. When we play to our strengths, we quickly find ourselves in the zone, where time passes, and we achieve at our best.

One of my top 5 is a thing called "WOO"—Winning Others Over. It means I love the challenge of meeting new people and winning them over.

I derive satisfaction from breaking the ice and making a connection with another person. I wondered if this would extend to winning over cheetahs.

I got on well enough—the cheetah I was stroking was purring in much the same way as a domestic cat, so I felt I must have been doing something right. Of course, it's one thing to interact with a young animal; I'm not so sure it would work the same way with a hungry adult!

Context matters: if there are serious shortcomings in an area that is vital to the role, then some action is needed. When designing those actions, you will have more success if you draw on the strengths to try to address the shortcomings.

Leadership Essentials: Values

We also recommend looking at the values that the individual has. If we can plan some improvements that harness both strengths and values, then the chances of success are greatly enhanced.

Values are those moral codes, or beliefs, that are embedded in our character through our family, education, and cultural influences that become an integral part of who we are.

I once had a coaching client who was being marked down for the way they managed people.

Knowing the individual, I was surprised, and when we talked about it, it transpired they were constantly late with handling and writing up the performance reviews of their people.

When probed, they confessed that they found the whole process to be arduous, bureaucratic, and inefficient. Through coaching, though, they had already revealed two resources to draw on; they connected well with people, loved having conversations, and were genuinely curious about others. The second thing to draw on was a strong value around developing people.

By using these two values, they stopped seeing the performance review through the lens of bureaucracy and were able to be more successful, both as a leader themselves and by developing others.

They also saw ways to improve the process and fed back to the organization changes that made the whole system work more effectively for everybody.

Working with an individual's strengths and values, rather than against them, sets people free to direct their energy, time, and resources more effectively.

Leadership Essentials: Develop the Team

Another way to approach the shortcomings in one individual is to look at the strengths of the team as a whole.

It is quite likely that someone else in the team is better equipped to do those tasks and indeed may even enjoy them.

However, imagine a team leader who, because she doesn't have a strength in a particular area, believes that the whole team thinks this way. Some people, in the service of being conscientious (a character value) may try and "protect" the team by hanging onto the task themselves, while, unbeknown to them, someone else would positively relish that challenge!

We can and should address peoples' shortcomings, but the most successful approach and the best use of our time is to focus on the strengths, not just in isolation, but with an eye to both the existing role and the next one in that individual's career.

We also need to analyze the needs of the role and compare that with the strengths of the individual. That might lead us to change aspects of the role as well as to design development actions that build on the strengths.

Those actions do have to look to the future; why wait until the individual is in the new post before equipping them to handle it well?

Look for opportunities to develop behaviors now that will improve their performance in their current role and maximize the chances of success in the next one.

In one organization I worked in, my PA was doing a fine job, and it was apparent that she had the potential to do more. Part of the role was to plan and organize training courses for building internal coaches.

Following discussions with her about her strengths and where her career might go, we agreed that she should attend the training course. It turned out she had a natural talent for this. The opportunity for her to use this skill fully was limited, in part because the organization was male dominated and, on average, older; not many of them would look to be coached by a much younger woman, even though we knew she could do a fine job.

She made an exceptional contribution on one training course, where we were introducing the skills to 16- and 17-year-old apprentices.

More importantly, the skills served her well as she moved up the ladder in HR, not just through formal coaching but also as a way of building a coaching style into her leadership and her interactions.

We need to deploy people in a way that is best for both them and the organization. That means we need to change our thinking about people and our expectations of them.

It's also important that we design our leadership competence models and the training we build around them in a way that reflects this reality.

The Evolution of Leadership

Let's look at it through the way leadership has evolved over the years.

Leadership isn't just about hierarchy, position, or status; it's about success and about people who take ownership and responsibility.

If you manage people or provide thought leadership, then a well-designed and well-researched model will help you be more successful. It will support your team to achieve more too, because the people who rely on your good work will benefit and your organization will be more successful.

In the middle of the last century, what we needed from our leaders was stability and efficiency. Organizations that were run well, with good continuity, efficient processes, and reliability, prospered. The pace of change was slow and business models were relatively simple.

Organizations had the luxury of time to analyze what they were doing and make incremental change, often trialed through pilots before scaling up. Many built on the successful models of automation and "assembly line" processes. They were able to grow through "time and motion" studies.

The approach to leadership in this generation is analogous to what many people see as the management side of the "management versus leadership" debate: doing things right and managing processes and systems, whereas "leadership" is doing the right things.

Leadership was often autocratic and commands were passed down. The managers in the hierarchy usually ran their teams in the same way as the company was run: the manager clearly in charge, giving orders. People weren't required to be creative; they were expected to follow orders and deliver. You were deferential to the people above you in the hierarchy and dictatorial to the people below you.

And in that environment, in that time and place, it was usually a recipe for success.

But the pace of change increased, complexity grew, and the luxury of time became scarcer.

This summary of leadership prior to VUCA World is, of course, a generalization. There have always been great examples of good leadership of the kind we would know today and organizations that were more successful as a result.

VUCA World and the Global Challenges

But there's no doubt we now live in an era tagged "VUCA": the era of volatility, uncertainty, change, and ambiguity.

We also face three challenges that the bestselling author Dan Pink cited in his book *A Whole New Mind*[3]: "Abundance, Asia and Automation." And, to quote General Petraeus,[4] there are now four global revolutions: IT, energy, manufacturing, and life sciences.

As consumers, we now have enormous choice. For organizations to survive, merely producing functional goods will never be enough. Look at the money spent on well-designed mundane objects such as an Alessi lemon squeezer, as an example.

For the West, the growth of Asia has increased competition, not only in the production of cheap goods (relative to home-produced goods), but also through growing numbers of highly educated knowledge workers.

The final challenge, automation, covers areas where traditional roles have been replaced through automation. This now covers areas such as legal documents that you can download for free or guides to conveyancing, undermining traditional jobs.

My own GP recently bemoaned the rise of Dr. Google and the impact it had on his relationships with his patients.

All of this shows how the world of work is changing radically. We can't stick to 20th century models of leadership; that too needs to change radically, because as leaders, managers, or business owners we will struggle to survive, let alone thrive.

We need people and organizations to be more creative, more adaptable, and to evolve more quickly than the competition.

This won't happen with hierarchical, command and control structures.

That worked when all we needed to know was how many widgets to make that day, and commands could come down the line, but it's very different today.

There's a parallel with evolution here; Charles Darwin is often misquoted in talking about the survival of the fittest.

What he said was: "It is not the strongest of the species that survive, nor the most intelligent, but the most responsive to change."

So organizations with a monoculture, rigid processes, and well-tuned systems work extremely well until change happens. Diversity, creativity, entrepreneurial qualities, and the occasional maverick may be more important.

It's certainly true that you are less likely to have people challenge the status quo or come up with radically new ideas if there is a culture of conformity.

This is especially true when combined with a blame culture.

We Need to Talk about the "F" Word: Failure

When failure happens, as it inevitably will, if the organization invests time and money in blame rather than learning from failure, people stop taking risks and organizations stagnate.

Failure isn't just about doubting ourselves; it's also about doubting others. These are vicious circles that play directly into the zero sum "lose/lose" mentality.

Failure paralyses and demotivates. Some people believe that we are motivated away from the fear of failure; that it spurs people on.

It's relatively normal for people to fear failure, and we're not suggesting that we ignore peoples' feelings, but rather that it be a temporary visit to the fear factory, instead of moving in permanently.

For some people, risk and challenge are spurs, and these feelings can be used as resources to motivate people and teams.

Our primary approach is to help people identify their vision of success; identify what they want to achieve, or identify what "good" or "success" looks like, or feels like. Orienting toward success is energizing and empowering.

If we're looking at blockages, or what's stopping us, our focus is on the problem. If we're orientated toward possibilities, new paths can open up in front of us.

With that backdrop, we need to find new ways of leading.

The Importance of a Well-designed Leadership 360

Prof Harry Schroder, a psychology professor at Princeton University, was fascinated about why some organizations were able to cope with increasing complexity and rapid change better than others.

As a result of his team's research, his book *Managerial Competence: The Key to Excellence*[5] was featured in Personnel Today's seven must read books.

He concluded that there are core skills common to organizations, regardless of professional or technical skills.

He found a series of "high-performance leadership behaviors" that are better indicators of success.

Part of the elegance of this model is that it applies equally (if differently) to a chief executive of a global multinational and to an individual managing no staff.

This means it is widely applicable.

When leadership is about people taking responsibility and taking ownership wherever they are in the organization and about people creating success for themselves and the team, the organization, and indeed in society as well, then we find the high-performance model supports this well.

What I especially like about it is the understanding that we are never going to be great at all 12 behaviors.

The rigorous research behind it allows us to benchmark the mix of behaviors we'd expect against the leadership complexity, from an individual contributor through a manager, a manager of managers, and right up to a global CEO.

There are three main elements to this model.

- The first is the behaviors themselves.
- The second is the level of performance for each behavior.
- The third is the relationship between the complexity of the role that you play and the mix of the first two elements.

The 12 behaviors fall into four clusters: Think, Involve, Inspire, Do.

The Think cluster covers the qualities we use to gather information and make decisions—how broadly we search for information when presented with a problem; how well we create robust ideas, ideally tackling more than one problem; and, finally, how flexible our thinking is, whether we have a plan B.

Involve is about getting other people on board; there's a great quote from one of my favorite shows, *The West Wing,* when the president seems not to be showing the leadership people expect.

The vice president says, "You know what they call a leader with no followers? Just a guy taking a walk."[6]

Involve is about skills that build empathy; getting teams to work well together and working one to one with people, coaching and mentoring them. (Plot spoiler: The president superbly outflanks his opponents and his poll ratings surge.)

Once we have explored great ideas and have a team around us, we need to **Inspire** them. People need confidence in themselves, and the leader has a huge role to play here. The leader also has to project confidence to the outside world. Communication skills are vital, and the subtle art of influencing comes into play here too.

Finally, for success to happen, the team actually have to **Do** something. This cluster is about taking action. It's also about continuous improvement; reviewing what worked well and what you might do differently in order to improve. Ultimately, it's about the focus you place on stakeholders, customers, patients, or service users, whatever term works for you.

There are five levels at which each behavior is assessed. The lowest is called negative; actions here have the potential to cause damage to the organization. The second level is just undeveloped; we don't notice anything. Level three adds value through the use of a behavior, and level four shows strength consistently and at a higher level, in a behavior.

What I like about the fifth level in this model is that it isn't about just doing more, but about creating systems and processes that encourage this behavior in everyone in the organization. It's about making it sustainable.

Finally, the more senior you are, and the greater leadership responsibility you have, the more you need to be demonstrating the behaviors, and at higher levels.

At the International Leadership Association Conference (2017), Petraeus talked about the leadership qualities now demanded by the revolutions and changes mentioned:

- Get the big policy and strategy ideas (**think**).
- Communicate the big idea (**inspire**).
- Oversee the delivery, tactics, and metrics (**do**).
- Create a formal process to revise big ideas (**do**).

It's understandable that an ex-army general would place less value on the **involve** behaviors, but armies have very particular ways of getting people on board, not all of which transfer well to civilian life.

The Schroder particular leadership behavior model also comes with a well-crafted 360. To beat our own drum, this is a model that we use internationally, with many client organizations. We have found it sufficiently all-encompassing and flexible enough for many organizations to adopt a variant of it.

Good design in a 360 ensures that the questions can be answered by someone who doesn't need to understand the technicalities of the behavior and the different levels at which someone can operate.

In other words, they don't need 120 pages of explanation.

It means that a process that is inevitably subjective, because it involves human beings, is made more objective.

Leadership Styles, as Distinct from Leadership Behaviors

In addition to the behaviors that leaders display, which are vital to success, people have different styles of leadership. Often this is just one default style, but the best leaders have a range of styles that they adapt to, depending on the context.

In their book *Primal Leadership/The New Leaders,*[7] the authors discuss six leadership styles based on emotional intelligence.

The styles are Visionary, Coaching, Democratic, Affiliated, Commanding, and Pacesetting.

As already argued, it will be hard for any one individual to be equally adept at all six styles. However, we should certainly strive to use more than just our default style.

This is especially true where the prevailing style in an organization is just one of these, because, quite often, it is the commanding style of leadership.

This is a cycle that needs to be broken.

Leadership styles pass down the generations as emerging leaders look to their elders for role models.

The VUCA World of work demands other styles of leadership, and all six styles have their place.

However, in our experiences the commanding and pacesetting styles are often overused.

It is possible to learn how to flex styles. The best way to do this is, again, to look at strengths and values.

Flexing helps identify which of the styles would be most easy to step into next. As people develop as leaders, there may be more opportunities to flex into, and increase the range of styles available.

Worksheet: Stimulus Questions

This chapter explores the, often unexpressed, assumption that a manager or leader has to be great in all areas of competence.

Leadership is a daily practice, a journey, not a destination. That means we practice, and sometimes fail, to be good leaders.

Nobody's perfect, yet hero figures are expected to succeed or risk being seen as "failures."

When reflecting on the content of this chapter, you may find it useful to answer these questions:

The Lens of Strengths

- What lens are we viewing people through, the lens of their strengths or of their shortcomings?

- How can you use their strengths in a way that is best for the organization, the team, and for them?

Personal Development Questions

- As a leader, what are my own strengths, beliefs, and default leadership style?
- Where would be the easiest place for me to develop and grow as a leader?

Influence

How can I influence the organization to promote some of these ideas?

Behavioral Mix

In your opinion, what's the mix of leadership behaviors your organization needs most:

- Thinking behaviors
- Influencing behaviors
- Inspiring behaviors
- Delivering behaviors

As above, use percentages to define what the mix might look like, for example, 25 percent for all 4, and so on.

Notes

1. M. Buckingham. 2008. "The Truth About You: Your Secret to Success", p.15, Thomas Nelson Inc.
2. J. Asplund, S. Agrawal, T. Hodges, J. Harter, and S.J. Lopez. 2007. Updated March 2014. *The Clifton Strengthsfinder® 2.0 Technical Report: Development and Validation* (Washington, DC: Gallup Inc.).
3. D. Pink. 2005. *A Whole New Mind* (Rolling Meadows, IL: Riverside Books).

4. D. Petraeus, October 2017, quoted from an interview at the International Leadership Association Conference (ILA), Brussels.

5. H.M. Schroder. 1989. *Managerial Competence: The Key to Excellence* (Dubuque, IA: Kendall/Hunt).

6. *The West Wing* (TV Series), "Shutdown" (season 5, episode 8), 2003, Dir. by Christopher Misiano, Writing Credits, Aaron Sorkin (created by), Mark Goffman (written by), Josh Singer (staff writer).

7. D. Goleman, R. Boyatzis, and A. McKee. 2002. *The New Leaders: Transforming the Art of Leadership into the Science of Results* (London, UK: Little Brown).

CHAPTER 10

Leaders—A Higher Lifeform?

I'm a leader not a follower. Unless it's a dark place, then you're going first.

—Unknown

Many years ago, I walked in to a splendid building in London, near to the Houses of Parliament. It was the headquarters of Her Majesty's Treasury, the financial hub of the UK government, and it was my first day in my first job that I thought was the start of a proper career. I had the grand job title of Executive Officer, and it was explained to me that I would be working to a Higher Executive Officer who, in turn, would be working to a Senior Executive Officer. There were several grades above that but given that progress from one grade to the next would take 4 or 5 years, I didn't see the point of remembering the detail.

There was great excitement that day in the office not, sadly, because I had joined, but because one of my new colleagues was due to retire. People clustered around her desk where she proudly displayed her medal, recently received from the Queen. She had worked in this government department all her life and had worked her way up several grades and was duly rewarded. It seemed that this was to be my destiny; if I wore a suit, turned up between nine and five, and did a good job, I too could aspire to a grander job title and a "gong."

I do not wish to denigrate the achievements of this person for the route that she took; at that time, it was commonplace to move up the hierarchy, to be paid more as she went up, and, by taking on leadership positions, to be rewarded in a way appropriate to the organization. I didn't have the right mindset to stick it out and lasted 6 months.

Outdated Paradigms

Those days of finding a job in a large paternal organization and staying there for life are long gone, but some of the attitudes that accompanied those paradigms have remained. The idea that we should start in a technical or professional role, increase our skills, and get paid a bit more for that until finally we are deemed so good at our job that the most sensible thing to do is to promote us into a management role, still prevails. That the only way to get more money and status is to move into management and then aspire to an even higher life form: The Leader.

When you look into the roots of the word manager you see it is derived from a 16th-century word *maneggiare*, which means "to control and train, especially horses."[1] It's no wonder that the people want to move out of management into leadership. In reality this procession through to nirvana is nonsense.

It's entirely reasonable that some people should want to move into management; it's a worthwhile and valuable discipline, in itself. It's also understandable that if you give people greater responsibility and they deliver against that, then they should be duly rewarded.

However, there are challenges with the "traditional" paradigm that I've outlined here. First, the distinction between managers and leaders is a false one that does not serve us in today's world of work. We've outlined in the previous chapter the leadership evolution that has happened, which means the traditional roles of manager and leader are blurred. We need people with both management skills and leadership skills, at many points in the organization. It's just the mix and the ratio of those two skills that will vary from role to role. In today's world, what we also need are people who are properly prepared, and empowered, to take ownership and take responsibility. The people who do that are leaders.

The problem, however, is we see leaders and managers as typically being roles that "other people report into." And so the only time that we give leadership training to people is once they've progressed some distance up that long ladder.

Leadership Essentials: Start Young

We need to start thinking about training people in leadership skills right from the very start of their professional careers. This is the argument supported by the UK Chartered Management Institute (CMI), who undertook a survey[2] with managers, management, and business students and 13 universities. Asked to assess the skills and behaviors of business school graduates, managers say the top strengths they see are:

- Managing innovation and digital technologies (83 percent somewhat or very strong)
- Curiosity and willingness to learn (79 percent)
- Inclusive and ability to work with different cultures (78 percent)
- Honest and ethical (78 percent)
- Financial skills (72 percent)

The weakest scoring areas are seen as being managing people, having difficult conversations, and taking responsibility . . . areas much in demand among employers for new managers.

The transition from the professional or technical skill into the manager or leader role is typically handled very poorly and often is driven by the wrong motive.

There are several outdated myths:

- That the only way to progress is through the management route;
- That leaders and managers are intrinsically worth more and contribute more than professional or technical experts.

A corollary of this is that people who want to earn more money have to step into management. We've all seen the problems that this can cause; classically you take the best salesperson and put him or her into a sales manager role. By doing so, not only have you just lost your best salesperson, but you may have put the worst possible person in charge of managing the people who now report to them.

There's an assumption that, despite having invested both money and time into creating good professionals, they can then step into management with hardly any training at all. The CMI call these people "accidental managers" because, although they have sterling qualities, they're allowed to fall into the role of manager/leader without preparation. Often, the most that they get is training by osmosis as it filters down from above them—some mentoring, perhaps, or being sent on a "presentation skills" course, as if that will sort it all out.

Leadership Essentials: Distinguish between People Leaders and Thought Leaders

We need to see management and leadership as highly regarded professions in their own right, *at the same time* acknowledging the value of those who remain in the professional or technical disciplines in which they excel. It just doesn't make sense to promote and reward those people who thrive in technical areas by turning them into people leaders. Some organizations recognize this and, rather than forcing them into the management of others career route, simply reward them for their thought leadership. And for those who thrive in the people leadership arena, perhaps it's time to recognize that it's a worthy profession in itself.

In the United Kingdom, only about 3 percent of people in management positions have got any formal qualification in the field; yet we allow these people to run our banks, hospitals, and airports. In contrast, CMI estimates that chartered managers,[3] CMI's gold standard accreditation, add more than £390,000 in value to their organization, and so the investment costs pale beside the payback. So, where we still have a need for managers and leaders, then the least we can do is invest properly in their development, ideally before we put them into a significant role.

We can also look at how we organize the tasks that the team have to do to make best use of all the skills of all the team. If we look at any role, then it really is just a collection of tasks that we have conveniently bundled into a single place and usually a single person. It doesn't have to be that way. We can break down the tasks that make up the role of manager and distribute them among the team. The concept of self-managed teams has been around for a while, and these work at their best when this approach of reallocating the managerial tasks is handled properly. These teams do, however, need a clear sense of purpose and direction; they need to understand what is required of them and where they fit into the organization. They need to deliver against targets.

Interestingly, if you ask teams to set their own objectives and targets, then typically two things happen. First, they tend to set more ambitious targets than you might and, second, they tend to overachieve against those targets. This is because people have a sense of ownership, responsibility, and commitment to the target, something that is lacking when the targets are externally set. There are other ways of structuring organizations that breakaway from the hierarchical model: networked organizations may be more appropriate and more flexible in today's world.

Leadership Essentials: Understand Motivation

Connected to this topic is the challenge to traditional ways of rewarding. Performance-related pay at an individual level is widespread. Yet there is a huge body of evidence that says that this is a very inefficient way of rewarding people and is unlikely to lead to the outcomes or behaviors that the organization intends. It can also have a negative impact: creating a climate of distrust and unhealthy competition. It leads organizations to create crazy rules and forbid people from talking to each other about their pay and reward packages.[4]

In a world where success is measured by creativity rather than the number of widgets produced, it's hard to objectively tribute success to different individuals in a fair way. Yet in most organizations, progress and success come as a result of great teams delivering, even though that doesn't necessarily mean that everybody's contribution is equal.

I once did an experiment with a team of five people when I called them into my office individually and said, "If I were to give you a sum of money to distribute as a bonus among yourselves how would you choose to spread that money around?" Four of them said that I should split equally among all of the team, but that Simon should get more as they all felt he was the best. Simon suggested a five-way equal split of the money.

People on the ground often have a better sense of where the value is being created, and we should learn to trust them more. We also need to address this notion that the only way to earn more is to move out of the job you do really well into a new job of management that we've never trained you for and for which you may be entirely unsuited.

We need to value the technical and professional contributions people make. This might mean paying your best technical people more than some of your managers. And that's hard to do if you still maintain a single hierarchy. In one organization I used to work in, to be promoted into a particular level of management, you were expected to manage people. In our small part of the organization, we changed this to promote technical people into that role and pay them more without giving them people to manage. It gave us flexibility and worked really well. A project manager who was looking for the best technical expert to work on the project might end up managing someone in his or her team who was being paid more than he or she was. But frankly, so what? The problem came a year or two later when a new departmental head challenged me as to why some people at that level were not managing staff; they reorganized and gave those people teams to manage. I jokingly suggested that they would do less damage to the organization if they lined the people up along wall and shot them, but my sarcasm fell on deaf ears. Our performance dropped, and we lost some great people.

Another danger with traditional, hierarchical thinking is the belief that the further up the organization you are, the more value you deliver, the better your decision making. You must be a higher life form.

Leadership Essentials: Nurture Creativity and Innovation

This takes us back to the risk of ego, particularly how often you will miss the great, value-adding ideas from people around you.

We are fortunate to live in a lovely village in the heart of England, close to the center of the UK motor industry. There are not so many mass manufacturing businesses these days; instead, there are specialist "advanced engineering" firms. They support projects like the Formula 1 teams in nearby Silverstone. Our neighbors in the village include several engineers, some of whom are retired. There's an admirable perfectionism about these people, though it makes for a very competitive environment sometimes. They also demonstrate the notion and value of transferable skills.

The annual produce exhibition allows those who have taken up gardening to show how meticulous preparation pays off. The scarecrow day, where villagers compete to create the most original scarecrow, taps into their imagination and innovation with some awesome constructions. I was chatting to one of our neighbors as he was bent over the bonnet of a sad-looking TR4. This was a sports car made by the Standard Triumph motor company in the early 1960s. It sold well in the United States and featured in the TV series *My Favourite Martian*. The appearance was great and contained many innovations, but the construction left something to be desired. The British car industry had started to lose its reputation for reliability. In conversation with Frank, I began to realize some of the reasons for it. It won't surprise you to know that poor leadership was one cause. I asked Frank what he planned to do to overcome the known design faults. He'd already found a better engine than the original; the footwell was a notorious rust spot, and he'd got around this by drilling some holes. But the most interesting part was when Frank started to talk about the chassis. He had been an apprentice engineer working on this very model when he started out on his career. He'd been asked to look at the design of the chassis and realized that it had an inbuilt flaw. It could easily buckle if the car had a relatively minor collision in just the wrong place. Frank went over his figures a few times and came up with a modification. Pleased with his work, he went to his supervisor, who immediately dismissed his ideas. His boss had been there a long time and thought he knew everything. He wasn't prepared to listen to this young apprentice.

The flawed design was similar to the modern method now used as a safety device for protecting pedestrians; so it was a good design in the right setting. The flawed chassis design was used until the company folded.

Worksheet: Stimulus Questions

In this chapter, we address the traditional assumptions about careers, and how organizations might need to change their approach to fit with VUCA World. We support the view that the leadership skillset needs to be introduced and developed in people as early in their career as possible. We explore the notion of leaders as "better than," in some indefinable way, managers or team members, when what we need in today's world of work are resourceful enablers who motivate and inspire each other, and, working together, get the job done.

Here's some questions you might want to ask yourself as you reflect on this chapter.

- What changes do you need to make in your mindset to get the best from all your people?
- What changes do you need to make in your organizational structure to get the best from all your people?
- Choosing a pilot role (or roles), if you broke it down to task level, how would you rebuild that role differently to be more effective?
- What impact might this have on where you invest in training and development?
- How might you restructure your reward systems to improve the outcomes you are looking for?

Notes

1. See, for example, https://www.etymonline.com/word/manage, (accessed May 15, 2018).
2. Chartered Management Institute. February 2018. *21st Century Leaders: Building Employability through Higher Education* (Report) (London, UK: CMI), op.cit.
3. Chartered Management Institute. 2015. *Mapping Management Excellence: Evaluating the impact of Chartered Manager* (London, UK: CMI).
4. See, for example, D. Burkus. 2016. *Under New Management* (New York, NY: Houghton Mifflin).

CHAPTER 11

Rose-Tinted View, or Interview?

In my country we go to prison first and then become President.
—Nelson Mandela

I love doing recruitment interviews. I've seen their benefits and found some great people along the way, some of whom have become enduring friends. However, I've also seen the downsides and wonder whether the interview is just an expensive method for looking at people through rose-tinted spectacles. It's time to explore alternatives to the traditional one-to-one interview, or interview panel, so that you can consider the options.

Back in the day my employer at the time ran a one-week training course for its interviewers and the pass rate was around 50 percent, and so they clearly took it seriously and invested in it heavily. One of the techniques we used was to create fictitious challenges to test the creativity of the people we were trying to recruit. One question I enjoyed using was telling people that they were in charge of the big switchover planned in driving habits; switching from driving on the left to the right. Their challenge in the interview was to plan this out and persuade me of the merits of their approach.

One of my favorite responses came from a candidate whose idea was to do the big cities first and leave the small towns and rural areas until later. When I asked what would happen on the boundaries of the big cities he picked up a piece of paper to draw his proposed interchange with flourishing sweeps of the pen. Then he stopped just at the point where he realized that a major pileup was inevitable. Let's be fair; the problem is probably impossible to solve, especially under interview conditions. My initial response, however, was that he should fail because of this. But we recruited him because, objectively, his marks from the panel overall showed that he deserved to pass. I admired his honesty and his reaction to spotting his mistake. And my initial "gut instinct" was wrong. I saw his work over the following couple of years and he was fine.

On another occasion, we had two people separately interview the candidates. We compared notes after both interviewing one individual. We'd gone through the objective process again and both of us scored him highly enough for a pass mark. But we both had reservations—in this case, for both of us, our gut instinct was telling us there was something "off" about the candidate. We chose not to offer him a job.

Leadership Essentials: Overcome Unconscious Bias

Over the years, I've been involved in different techniques that we used to recruit people, and we know from all the literature that there are flaws with many of them. And yet we still persist because it is important to get a good technical and cultural fit for new people. It's a win–win. I've done interviews with people who claim they know within the first 10 seconds when a candidate walks through the door whether they are going to get the job or not. I've heard people say "despite all the interview training, we simply recruited the people we liked."

I know from my own experience that, however objective I try to be, unconscious bias still comes in. I worked really hard when recruiting one person; as a white middle-aged man who knew not a lot about HR, I was proud of the fact that I'd recruited a young person of color with an HR degree. How could I have picked somebody any more different? However, in her first few weeks she did the Myers Briggs assessment and it turned out she was exactly the same as me. So much for "objectivity." Again, the issue isn't that "objectivity" is better than the combination of experience and knowledge that we call "instinct"; it's that we build self-awareness, stay alert to the possibilities of bias, and work in pairs or panels to make better selection decisions.

There have also been some great improvements over the years in the way that recruitment takes place, in a desire to remove unconscious bias. In the early 1950s, the Boston Symphony Orchestra wanted to improve the ratio of women to men in the orchestra and started to do auditions with a screen between the musician and the interview panel. The theory was that by only hearing the musicians play, the panel would choose the best musicians regardless of gender. Surprisingly, at first it made no difference. Then they made a subtle change; they asked the musicians to take off their shoes before walking onto the stage; it transpired that the judges could hear the sound of the heels that the female musicians wore as they walked on stage and this had biased their judgments. After this change, recruitment to the orchestra was pretty much 50–50 male to female.

There has been much written about techniques to remove bias, such as removing names from CVs, removing the names of universities from your qualifications, and excluding addresses and dates of birth. All of these are excellent ways to maximize the possibilities of hiring a more diverse workforce.

Although all these are good steps to take, if we continue to have the interview to be the final arbiter, to carry the most weight, then we will find it harder to achieve the objective of a more balanced workforce.

We all have biases.

Unconscious Bias in Our Language

The next step in this revolution toward a more diverse workforce uses technology to address our unconscious linguistic biases. It starts with the recruitment advert and job description.[1] Apparently some words bias toward attracting male candidates and some toward female. "Managing," for example, is a "male" word; and "running" is the "female" equivalent. "Important" is "male" and "meaningful" female. Or, to put it another way if a job was described as "an important management role," it would attract fewer women, which biases it toward male applicants.

The technological approach is known as "augmented writing" and is being pioneered in the United States and the United Kingdom. According to Textio, a company providing an online augmented writing service for job roles, "high-scoring companies" attract "25% more qualified candidates, more candidates from under-represented groups, and fill jobs faster."[2] The "scoring" is on a 1–100 rating, where 90 or more is considered high scoring. It's not just corporate clichés that drag down a job advert by appealing more to men than to women, but words like "stakeholder" are less appealing to people of color. Yet ironically, these words are trying to be inclusive. Using the Textio system, we put excerpts from this book through the system, identifying it as an "HR role for London, UK." Some excerpts (primarily written by Bob) had a "male" bias and some (written by Helen) were more "female." Although these technologies have the power to improve equality and diversity, they also have the power to deliberately discriminate against groups, even if this means skewing the job advert and missing out on the diversity dividend.

Leadership Essentials: Address Misperceptions

We all create impressions, and we are all influenced by them. It reminded me of a time in my earlier career as a manager when someone I knew came back to work for me. I remembered him especially from his rather drunken 21st birthday party and the image of him from there was still with me. Of course, he had by now matured into a great person, but it took me a while to reset my opinion.

I hear that Facebook has a similar impact when people post "the morning after the night before" pictures and messages today. The brain seems to store images in our long-term memory: the faces of people we've met along with the opinions we've formed of them. This includes even our opinions of people we've never met.

Think of a famous person—my guess is you have a view of what he or she is like, and an opinion of him or her, even without ever meeting that person. When you meet someone new, the brain flicks through its folder of images and, if it finds a match, it assigns the same characteristics from the person in memory to the person you've just met.

I was talking to a group recently about the importance of perceptions. As a leader, people will form opinions about you, often on the basis of the scantest of information. We can influence that perception. We always have an impact when we walk into a room, especially if we are the leader. Too often, it's not one we have chosen. And people read things into our behavior. They extrapolate from the smallest frown and make the assumption that you are ritually bad tempered. So it's important to choose the impact you want to have—just as true of the interviewer as the interviewee, as part of the job these days is to sell the company to the interviewee.

Author Adam Bryant talked about this in his book *The Corner Office*[3] on the basis of his interviews with CEOs for his column in the *New York Times*. He mentions one CEO who has a favorite interview question— "What misperceptions do people have of you?" This is interesting enough, but it is just a set up for the next question: "What is the difference between a misperception and a perception?" I want to say that a misperception is when people are wrong, but really there is no difference.

I had a great conversation with one of the leaders in an international organization we work with. He was talking about a briefing he had once on the customs and etiquette in a particular country: "They told me to be careful because in that country, people didn't like to be seen to lose face." I asked him who in the world actually enjoys losing face? On our leadership development programs, when we ask for volunteers to participate in a front-of-the-room exercise, in the United Kingdom, we get told that this might work in America, where they are "more forward." My experience is that in the United States, there is just as much shuffling of feet and lack of eye contact as in the United Kingdom. The difference is that when someone does finally crack, in the United States the rest of the group applaud, whereas in the United Kingdom they wipe their brow and exclaim "Phew!"

Collaborative Hiring

The concept of collaborative hiring is becoming more commonplace. By engaging a wider group of people in the recruitment process, we can address unconscious bias, even if we can't eradicate it altogether. We may also cancel out the different biases that we have. A popular sandwich shop chain in the United Kingdom, Pret a Manger, adds another step at the end of a traditional process of vetting an online application, a telephone interview, and a face-to-face meeting. It is called the "graduation day". Here, the applicant spends a morning working alongside the team he or she hopes to join, and the final decision is made by that team. It's still far from perfect; the team members are very likely to recruit someone in their own image but, given the small space they work in and the frantic pace of the job, perhaps the ability to get on with the rest of the team outweighs other factors.

The BBC once ran a program called *Who's the Boss?*[4] In this show, applicants had to carry out a number of tasks while being filmed. In one episode, a potential logistics manager had to plan a delivery route and then go out with the driver to follow that route. Although the candidates knew they were being filmed, they weren't aware until the final day that *everybody* else in the company was watching. The film clips were seen by the whole company who ultimately decided who would get the job. It made for entertaining television and, like other collaborative hiring ideas, has the potential to average out individual unconscious biases.

Another technique used to narrow down the field is the use of psychometrics. When used correctly, these can prove to be hugely valuable.

It's Not Only Humans Who Are Biased

An airline client, who is one of the fastest growing airlines in the world, started to use psychometrics when recruiting for cabin staff around 10 years ago. It first analyzed the factors that it believed would be most important in the personality characteristics of those staff. One of the key elements was flexible thinking—both the belief that there could be an alternative and then the ability to craft those alternatives. It used a self-report personality test called 16 PF as one of those factors pointed to this quality of flexible thinking.

A safety culture is vital in the airline industry and having a plan B in the event of a crisis is seen as critical. However, one area where it doesn't work so well is when we use tools to profile successful people in the role and then recruit against that profile. This technique is increasingly used not just with psychometrics but also with leadership competence frameworks. The flaw I see here is the assumption that just because one person operates in a particular way and is successful, then the route to success is to emulate that person's approach.

A coaching client aspired to a particular managerial role. In that organization, there were about 40 similar roles. She confessed to being reluctant to even think about taking on the role because she couldn't see how she could behave and lead in the same way as the incumbents. As we moved through the coaching, she noticed three things: the majority of the incumbents were male; the majority of the people they managed were male; and most of those 40 managers were leading and managing in a similar way. They managed in ways not just similar to each other, but also similar to the layer of management above them. As we talked it through, she outlined what her approach would be, how she would deal with the teams, and how she might manage upward differently. When she realized she didn't have to manage in the same style as the incumbents, she became quite liberated and animated about new ways of fulfilling those duties.

If the organization had profiled those 40 managers and looked at the ones who were more successful versus the less successful, and had then tried to recruit to that profile, she wouldn't have stood a chance. I'm not saying that those successful men were doing a bad job—far from it. The point is that she and they can successfully do that same job, but in very different ways. And the profiling approach would have mitigated against her. This is a fundamental principle inherent in our thinking around leadership. The debate about whether leaders are born or made is the wrong debate. We believe that most people can lead. They do so much better when they understand and develop their leadership behaviors and their style, and it's certainly true that some leaders will be more appropriate than others depending on the context. But they have to lead from their beliefs and values. This is about authenticity and integrity—leading from who they already are, rather than pretending to be, or trying to be, someone else.

What Do We Mean by "Authentic" Leadership?

One of the enduring hero myths is that of hiding their true identity—usually with a mask. Revealing that identity is usually kept to a very small circle of people—think Superman's girlfriend—which tends to be a life-threatening role in fiction! Hiding your identity in superhero films is usually a metaphor for not showing your "weaker" emotional side (notice that it's usually the girlfriend who gets to find out the "truth").

When we talk about authentic leadership, we are normally talking about character: ethical and moral approaches based on genuine relationships; about being open and positive. Our definition would extend this to include being authentically themselves: our whole, emotional, ragged, flawed selves. So, although there are approaches you can take to improve the interview process, and to more accurately select the people you interview in the first place, the concept itself is flawed. There are better, more effective, and more efficient ways to find the right person for the job. It is still in essence a beauty parade. In the same way as examinations in the educational system lead us to raise up people who are good at exams into elite status, the interview process will lead us to select people who are good at interviews. These are not necessarily the people who are best for the job.

When presented with two candidates, one internal and one external, we tend to favor the external candidate because all we have seen of that person is the 1 hour when they are on show. We already know a lot about the internal candidate and yet, surprisingly, this often weighs against them. It's not logical, especially if that internal candidate has been doing the job and is already delivering well. One solution is to find more ways to observe how that person would actually perform in the job. There are various ways we can do this.

One way is to use development or assessment centers. We design a day in a fictitious company where participants operate at a higher level than at which they are currently working. They face a number of challenges that enable us to observe the leadership behaviors they exhibit in this artificial environment. There are other variants on this, such as the Situational Judgment Tool, where theoretical examples are presented and multiple-choice options are given to the candidate. This has merit but is not as rigorous as the development center. Some of our clients use it as a filter to determine who they send to the development or assessment centers.

Another option is work shadowing, where a trained assessor will observe the individual in a range of activities in his or her current job. Then there's a behavioral event interview, where we talk through experiences that the person has already had and see how he or she approaches them. Work shadowing and behavioral event interviews are both useful in that we can see the leadership behaviors they are displaying. The obvious downside is that it takes place in the familiar environment of their current job. Another option is to find ways to try them out in the more senior role in a way that is both supportive to them and with minimal risk to the organization. Simple approaches include temporary cover for a senior vacancy or standing in for the manager while they are on holiday.

Although these things happen regularly, it is less common for them to be actively used as a way of assessing the person in that role. Most people "acting up" or providing holiday cover tend to have a natural fear of doing anything other than keeping things ticking over for that short period of absence. However, where clear agreements between the incumbent and the stand-in happen, for example, with decision-making boundaries, their role in meetings, and so forth, this task can turn into a real developmental opportunity.

One organization I worked with had a talent pool of 100 people. We decided to accelerate their promotion, as waiting for opportunities to arise was not moving them on fast enough. We set out a challenge. We asked them to come to us with an idea for a role, either an existing or new one they felt should be created, that was two levels further up the hierarchy than where they currently were. (This was an organization that still had quite a few levels of management before delayering became popular.) Where the proposal was plausible, we formally promoted them one grade up, then monitored their performance closely over the next 6 months. We put support mechanisms in place, such as a mentor and a coach, with the potential to promote them to the grade two levels up on the basis of their performance in that role. Our belief was that this would have a number of benefits: It would encourage the talent pool, which was not moving very quickly, to believe that they truly were being thought of as talent.

The second advantage was that they may find some new and different way of approaching the work that hadn't been thought of. In practice, it proved quite daunting and, despite encouragement, only one person out of the 100 took up this challenge. Yes, they struggled for 6 months but they persevered and, by the end of that time, were doing a great job and were fully deserving of their promotion. One out of a hundred doesn't sound much; but we deemed it a success for more reasons than just one person's experience. An unexpected side effect was that we were able to critically review the other 99 people in the talent pool.

We concluded that many were there for the wrong reasons. Some were the blue-eyed boys of their managers (they were mainly "boys"). Some were the truly valuable technical experts, and their manager thought that by "rewarding" them with a place in the talent pool, they might stay a little longer working for them. It led to a wholesale review of how we selected people for the talent pool.

One organization that we work with has strict rules about how long people can stay in a particular post and so they rotate people, even to the point that you may take over your boss's position and they may revert to being one of your staff. They are fully trained and prepared for the role. And they have the great asset of somebody who has done the job before.

In some organizational cultures, this may challenge some peoples' egos to accept this rotation. And it may take time to see this as both a usual step, and the normal way to distribute leadership and create a more abundant leadership capability in the organization.

No interview or recruitment process is ever perfect. Some people say that automated recruitment is one way forward as it is less subjective. Until you read about all the ways that applicants are being "guided" to beat the system, my recommendations are that you recruit as a team, rely on your experience and a diversity of recruitment methods (not just the "beauty parade"), and keep up to date with new ways of thinking about leadership and new ways that people will game whatever system you use.

Worksheet: Stimulus Questions

This chapter explores the way we recruit and interview people. We question whether interviews are just an expensive method for looking at people through rose-tinted spectacles. So here are a few questions to ask yourself:

- Where have I shown unconscious bias or inherent prejudice in my hiring process?
- What might we do to reduce the bias in the advert or role description?

- How can we improve selection beyond the classic interview?
- What is a safe, but still challenging, way to try people out in high-level jobs?
- How can I support people to break out of the traditional molds of leadership that they see around them?
- What needs to change in the organization for people to feel safe to try out the new, more engaging leadership approaches?
- How might we build a coaching and mentoring culture in our organization?

Notes

1. D. Silverberg. n.d. "Why Do Some Job Adverts Put Women Off Applying?" https://www.bbc.co.uk/news/business-44399028, (accessed June 20, 2018).
2. Textio.com/products video (accessed June 20, 2018).
3. A Bryant. 2011. *The Corner Office* (New York, NY: HarperPress).
4. BBC. 2016. "Who's the Boss?", https://www.bbc.co.uk/programmes/b0725xkj/episodes/guide, (accessed May 2, 2018).

CHAPTER 12

Wanted: Sharp People and Well-Rounded Teams

The problem with being a leader is that you're never sure if you're being followed or chased.

—Claire A. Murray

There are four key things we know about heroes from cinema experiences. We've addressed the cape issue and the hidden identity. The third is less obvious: to succeed you need to go "up." Whether that's climbing the outside of a tower block, flying up, or using a jet pack, up is the way to go.

We echo this myth in our organization structures and encourage people to climb the ladder of success. What gets conveniently ignored is that it's like the board game, snakes and ladders. The time will come when you land on a square where the only way is down and out. And in today's world of flatter organizational structures, it seems like the ladders have been taken away. All that's left are the snakes.

"Excuse My Dust"[1]

The fourth central story is that superheroes may have flaws, but they succeed because they care, in contrast to the cold antiheroes who live in highly mechanized lairs and certainly don't care about little old ladies. We carry this part of the story into organizations when we say that we need "well-rounded people," equipped with all the social skills. This "rounding out" tends to mean fixing peoples' limitations and, where possible, turning them into strengths.

Organizations aren't so forgiving of the flaws, however, because they create waves of unrest. What they want are sociable people with super-powers of empathy and the competence to motivate others. The reality is that what they get are people with flawed humanity, who might be forgiven those flaws as long as they continue to deliver heroically. The quote (or misquote) "pardon my dust" by poet Dorothy Parker may have referred to signs noted on early motor cars. The drivers were aware that these new machines had the flaw of putting out pollution. It's a para-dox: on the one hand, the risk is that the flaws alienate; they push other talented people away. On the other hand, acknowledging that we're all flawed, and acceptance of our own imperfections, can make it easier to accept those flaws in others. Once an individual has shown the right attri-butes in the development phase, they need to gain experience, to be able to deliver at their best. At the same time, we need to support their skill development so that they empathize with, and motivate, others to deliver their best, too. After all, leadership is a practice, not a theory.

One way to achieve more is to take personal responsibility down to the lowest level in the organization, and in this way, leaders don't need to feel like lonely superheroes, denying their true identity. This "warts and all" approach may not be the prettiest. We want to present our best face—whether to colleagues, customers, or the boss. But it's exhausting, and isolating.

A team doesn't have to be a group of people with a leader at the top; it could be a group of people with an enabler, a project driver or facilitator, who just happens to be the first point of contact for management information—for seeding ideas or creating a forum for discussion and debate. It is also where everyone takes responsibility, for contributing each person's strengths, for delivery, and for bringing out the best in each other. If the organization values these sideway moves, career progression doesn't have to be only upward. It's a very different definition of "leadership"—a world away from developing "well-rounded individuals." Instead, it requires sharp individuals who, together, are willing to make up a well-rounded team, and not just to create the team but to dissolve it and reorganize when the time comes. In starlings, it's called "murmuration." It's the time, in early evening, where thousands of birds flock together and perform the most amazing aerobatics. They are more than stunts; it's a security and information activity combined. In humans, friction arises because perceptions of how leaders and teams could be, "should" be, and nostalgia for how it used to be are all different.

The Ultimate Deployment Tool: Leaders Developing Future Leaders

The scholarship of Harold M. Schroder and his research team is worth retelling here as it's a fundamental underpinning to the way we need to define, discover, develop, and deploy leaders in today's complex and uncertain world. This work inspired our leadership definition of context plus applying high-performing behaviors and a leadership style, relevant to that context. The team first looked at the literature on "trait" leadership—based on the hero or "great man" theory of leadership.

As you'd expect, we have an issue with any definition that excludes 51 percent of the world's population, but that was the world they inhabited back then. They also looked at situational influences and peoples' responses to those. The conclusion that led to the formulation of high-performing behaviors, or competences, was that a combination of the two is needed. They saw that leaders needed to be flexible because, of course, situations in different organizations are not constant; they're unpredictable (even within an organization) and require different responses. The research team also predicted the increasing pace of change in the new technological era, its volatility, and uncertainty. This means that leaders need to flex their behaviors to succeed in uncertain and ambiguous situations. They saw the need for leadership development to be highly relevant to the daily life of leaders and for support to be put in place to ensure that they could be successful in those shifting situations.

For us this means taking some of the in-post learning and development support out of the classroom and as close to the coalface as possible, helping people to see the constants in the shifting VUCA World, and, more importantly, helping them to flex when there don't seem to be any constants.

Most radical of all, Schroder saw every future leader as having a development plan.[2] Firstly, he wanted to go further than simply "rounding out" limitations. Secondly, he wanted people to be aware of their own strengths and increase the contribution they made as leaders from those positions of strength. Thirdly, he wanted leaders and managers to capitalize on the "strengths of other workgroup members."[3] His team's work was ahead of its time and remains so today. Yet the world around us shows us that it's increasingly relevant because whereas Schroder researched in anticipation of VUCA World, today we're living it.

Team and Leadership Murmurations

We see this flexibility when new organizations take strategic decisions on what they will insource and what they will outsource. We see this when they plan which organizations they will partner with to deliver goods and services and which goods and services will be created in house. We don't think twice about buying a car that has been assembled under a brand name—yet most of the components have been supplied using "just in time" logistics services from many different sources around the world. We're happy to choose one brand of smartphone over another, regardless of whether most of the components come from the same factory, and that brand B will have the same functionality. These arrangements are possible because component purchasers are willing to outsource responsibility and performance delivery to a third party. It's another way of devolving responsibility to the lowest level and relies on three key elements: quality, security, and communications.

Our own organization, the Forton Group, has grown in this way. Like many agile organizations, we have international partnerships with expert partners on four continents, who rely on us to set and maintain quality leadership and coaching standards. Even if the organization size and structure permits, promotion into a new and even more responsible role may not be the answer.

There's a structural step that organizations can take to support the experience development. And, in today's flatter organizations, gaining wider experience—for example, by moving sideways, or diagonally, may be better deployment answers. Many organizations already do this, alongside other development activities, such as coaching, mentoring, and PALS (Peer Action Learning Sets, initially tutor facilitated) already mentioned.

I well remember my management training, a million years ago (!), which essentially consisted of working in each department in the company to gain an understanding and experience of what went on. I still feel great sympathy for many of those departmental leaders and managers having to put up with this person who clearly didn't have the aptitude for their department's technical specialty. And I am grateful to this day for the opportunities they gave me. I suspect I wasn't the only person to sigh with relief when I found my niche in a mix of business planning, promotions, procurement, and facilities management. I was given the freedom to take significant decisions; I was supported by the extended network of the wider organization, and I discovered the power of strong business relationships—even when negotiations got tense. I also remember, as a woman, having role models around me against whom I could compare my own career path—what I did (and didn't want) in my future. Many years before the "Lean In" phenomenon, I negotiated my own pay rise and managed procurement budgets in the millions. Yet I gave all this up because my career trajectory took me to University as a mature student. "Up" was not what I wanted.

Gaining experience can mean sideways or even diagonal moves across the organization. With flatter structures in today's organizations, it's also important to manage expectations of what "up" could look like. There was a period, in the 1980s and 1990s, when expectations of rapid promotion were the norm. Wage inflation went alongside expectation of greater status and responsibility. Before that, wages rose slightly each year and promotion was an occasional possibility, not an expectation. In today's economy, wages rises and promotion expectations are dampened, with organizations expected to do more for less. Yet the desire to rise "up" continues. Partly because the pay gap between the lowest and the highest has grown ever wider, with CEO pay ratios of 300 times the "worker pay" being quoted.[4]

It's not just that greed is an unattractive attitude; it also takes the focus away from the current role into positioning for exposure, attention, and future promotion. The desire to be seen to succeed, as solo hero, exceeds the desire to achieve as a team.

When to Stretch and Challenge?

So when is the right time to support people to dive into the deep end? It is when technical experts show strong people management skills and demonstrate promise through the development program. Moving them into a people manager role might be exactly the challenge they're looking for. Conversely, some technical experts will never show the attitude or aptitude for people management. In fact, it might be detrimental to good team work, morale, and delivery.

A strong project manager may need to develop his or her commercial or financial awareness and would welcome the opportunity to gain experience in that area of the organization. This notion may alarm some readers. The idea of "letting someone loose" as a manager in a commercial section without a strong background in that area doesn't sit well with some people. Another way to support people to get this kind of pan-organizational experience, at low risk, is to use corporate social responsibility activities to gain wider experience.

For example, there's nothing like the single-minded focus of a fundraising target and plan to develop innovation and commercial awareness. Knowing that a hospice or a children's educational facility depends on these efforts is a great way to unlock people's resourcefulness. They can gain real-world experience at the same time.

Again, there are risks. People need to appreciate that a charity isn't a playground to try out their pet theories but a real-world challenge with vulnerable people depending on their skills and strengths. When we couple leader deployment with devolved operational responsibility to the lowest possible level, as recommended by Schroder, it's clear that these leaders are there not to be operational experts but to support and guide team members to succeed.

It's one of the biggest challenges in our leadership development programs—and one we throw in early on. We encourage people to explore a model that delegates the task and supports devolved accountability and responsibility to team members. If quality standards, security, and communication (the bedrock of risk management) aren't in place, it's easy to see that this is a scary place for new leaders to be in.

Step Away from the Desire to "Know" and to "Tell"

It challenges peoples' sense of themselves, particularly their need to know and tell—to show that they're the expert—especially when they first step into those roles. More experienced managers see the value of asking questions and being more coach like or mentor like. They know they'll get more from their teams in this way. At the heart of the challenge is stepping into the zone of "not knowing." It takes someone willing to have a "beginner's mind" and the humility to know that team members have expertise that the person doesn't.

We're back to the willingness of the leader or manager to drop his or her egos and leave the hero myth behind. What both amazes and amuses us is that, with every group we work, at least one participant has a story to share about someone he or she knows who doesn't have all the answers yet is still prepared to tell others what to do.

The Myth of the Well-Rounded Leader

So let's challenge the myth of the need for a well-rounded leader. Our cinematic heroes have frail grandmothers to care for and whole populations to protect. Thankfully, they're given superpowers that help them achieve these objectives and keep the world safe for humanity. For the rest of us, developing our empathy and sociability is heroic enough. We don't need to have all the answers, but just the skill and humility to know who to ask and how to ask in ways that creates collaboration and better answers.

In Schroder's terms, in interpersonal search it's important to "find out what others are thinking and feeling." This notion of collaborative team building in this way is still a radical idea today. We're used to having a team of people around us—and there are many leaders and managers who resist the idea of virtual teams—it comforts people to be surrounded by "their" people.

The idea of creating cohesion across functions is still unusual, resisted by many managers. The notion that a job is a series of tasks, rather than a fixed role, is also challenging. The idea that tasks and roles might flex during the lifetime of a project is anathema to those people who like fixed timescales and budgets and clear job titles on the Gantt chart. We argue that organizations need sharp people leading "well-rounded teams." That is, individual leaders who feel confident enough to lead teams through uncertainties and sudden turns. They build collaboration by consulting with people around them by **not** having all the answers. It takes a sharp and confident brain to do this. Under pressure, the pull is back to "command and control" and create an air of confidence (often false) by barking out commands and getting people into action. This is because, yes, people do feel more confident and in control when they take action. Even in these more urgent situations, maintaining a questioning and learning culture creates opportunities to embed better ways of working, rather than just one person's preferred system. This is about getting to the right actions, via the right decisions. The leader must be sharp enough to stop and engage the team in thought, before getting into organized actions. This is the place for reflective practice. Reflection needs time and space. Taking time to reflect is an investment, not a weakness. This process of shared thinking works particularly well in the face of ambiguity. Encouraging the exploration of different options and looking at different perspectives will support clearer decision making. Those heroic movie moments when a protagonist declares "you have no choice!" are particularly irritating because they support the notion of binary thinking, which is rarely helpful in complex situations.

Yes, in puzzles there are single solutions. But, as we discussed at the beginning, VUCA World isn't like that. So supporting leaders to succeed in this environment means accepting the reality of ambiguity in practical ways. It particularly helps at times of volatility. The risk is that people will engage in stop/start behaviors that throw projects and programs off course: first going one way; then another—prioritizing one course of action; then stopping that and prioritizing another.

I remember working to a deadline in the days when software developers wrote their own code. The project combined a number of venue seating and payment and booking operations that are common today, but then were cutting edge. Of course, the team members had the skills to deliver, but they also were overconfident about their ability to deliver in the available time and underprepared to accept the complexity. They also wanted to throw away the manual system, in a dramatic, boat-burning moment. I watched as the people supposedly "championing" the project ran for cover and my line manager trotted out his "back protection" routine. We delivered, with days to spare. But it taught me a valuable lesson in discovering who your real supporters are, as distinct from the people who are meant to be. Thirty years later, there are people who still have my back in delicate international challenges and continue to give their support when asked.

The Power of Asking as a Way of Supporting

Sharp individuals with enough influence and the willingness to consult with their colleagues in times of volatility can ensure that the leadership team work together for the benefit of the whole organization. When done well, this approach can tap into a range of perspectives. It particularly plays well to the strengths of people, often introverts, who prefer to be asked for their ideas and opinions, rather than offer them. It also balances out the exaggerated influence of those (extroverts) who speak up first, or most often, offering their ideas in meetings, without giving space to others.

The greatest payback from this collaborative approach is the support between leader and team. It's inspirational to hear great ideas from others when we connect with the whole team and tap into their experience. It also promotes a genuine sense of empathy that we really are "all in it together."

I once worked in a 1,500-strong department. We had a poor reputation and a new manager came in to "sort us out." One of his first actions was to get the top 50 managers together for a meeting. This spanned a couple of levels in the hierarchy, and so we were a little surprised when he announced we were all now working as direct reports to him. In that first meeting, he asked,

> *"OK, so who is interested in how we run the department's finances?"*
> About ten people put their hands up.
> *"Great. You're the finance committee. Now, who is interested in people?"*
> I put my hand up along with another ten or so.
> *"Great. You're the people committee."*

His overarching message was

"I'm here if you need me, but I expect you to just crack on and do those roles."

We had all the support and power we needed—he genuinely had delegated and not abrogated. The reputation of the organization improved. And my new career in leadership development was launched. Twenty years later, we still meet up socially every 3 months or so. Not everyone, but many people still show up. We chatted about his approach at one of those social events. He said he'd been advised that the best way to sort the unit out was to sack the top 50 and start again, but that was never really an option. He had also been told that he wasn't allowed to have so many direct reports, but he decided to do it anyway. What he achieved was to tap into what we enjoyed doing and play to our individual strengths; at the same time, he encouraged us to work together as a fully functioning team. My recollection is that we had fun while also taking the work seriously, and this once-failing department became a central pillar of the organization.

Whatever the exact model in your organization, the general direction is clear. It's what 21st-century workplaces demand. There's no longer a single career path leading to a seat on the Board. Rather it's a series of several, very different career options, from operational delivery to technical expert, to tutor or coach, to leader or manager, at each step applying a range of leadership behaviors to keep the team on track. Once we can envisage this flexibility for ourselves, we can also find new ways to energize others, holding hold high expectations about other peoples' potential and the expectation that they will take ownership and responsibility for what they contribute. Seeing the role of the leader as someone providing resources, support, and feedback to team members, rather than being some kind of higher level of life form, set apart from the rest. These flatter hierarchical structures also challenge the notion of automatic right to a promotion, or even to pay increases or bonuses based purely on experience.

What "Experience" Really Means

It's an old adage to ask whether someone with 20 years' of experience is really more of an expert, or just someone with one year's experience twenty times. The intention isn't to denigrate experienced people, but rather to challenge what we reward—because where money is concerned if you allocate a financial value to a behavior, people will demonstrate it. It's at the heart of transactional leadership—"if you do enough of this, then we'll reward you with more money." Some people will plot their moves out on the board game, which is your organizational structure, purely on the basis that they're heading for where they perceive the best combination of challenge, power, and reward lies for them. It's a key reason why women (generally) don't thrive in this masculine model of hero leadership. Because (and I generalize here) this kind of "gaming the system" is meaningless and unfulfilling. Sharp leaders will use empathy to find out what does matter to people who prefer a different kind of transaction and help shape their roles to meet those career aspirations. Just because some people have competitive tendencies in their careers doesn't mean everyone does. Getting to the heart of peoples' career drivers can bring out the best in people—again, tapping into and releasing their potential. This "manager as coach" approach uses coaching skills like empathy, listening, and powerful questioning to uncover and support peoples' career aspirations. And it supports them to deliver their best in their current role.

It's time to get off the snakes and ladders board. To challenge the myth that says we develop people to go up the organization. It's time to give people a broader range of options, including to go across or diagonally. Yet challenging this myth demands change in other areas. If the organization structure is flatter, then responsibility needs to be devolved to the lowest possible level. Easier to do when tasks are outsourced—because necessity demands it—than when the tasks remain within the team. Too often the leader will cling on to responsibility and neglect to tap into the team's talents and experience. Collaborative, inclusive, abundant leadership depends on skills of empathy and understanding others, which is why a simple place to start is by asking others for their opinions and experience.

This challenge shifts the role of the leader from someone who is expected to know everything and tell others what to do, to someone who can invite the opinions of others, without the expectation or burden of having to come up with all the answers. It challenges the myth of developing a cadre of well-rounded leaders and enables them to be more themselves: sharp people leading well-rounded teams.

Worksheet: Stimulus Questions

This chapter explores the notion of "well-rounded people" and the desire to iron out the wrinkles, rather than accept sharp individuals who, working together, are willing to make up a well-rounded team. So here's a few questions to ask yourself as you review this chapter:

- What generic headings might go into a personal development plan for all our staff?
- How might we stretch and challenge people?
- How do we deal with "sharp people" in our organization? And how might we support them better?
- How might we really get the best from people, without putting them into a "talent pool" or onto a pedestal?

Notes

1. "Excuse my dust" a suggested epitaph by poet Dorothy Parker quoted in *Vanity Fair* magazine, 1925.
2. P.150 H.M. Schroder, *Managerial Competence.*
3. Ibid., p. 32.
4. P. Hodgson. June 22, 2015. "Top CEOs Make More than 300 Times the Average Worker," http://fortune.com/2015/06/22/ceo-vs-worker-pay, (accessed January 5, 2018).

CHAPTER 13

Pulling It All Together

Coming together is the beginning.
Keeping together is progress.
Working together is success.

—Henry Ford

Abundant leadership is a vision for an inclusive, empowering way to better lead and manage teams. It's about aligning personal, team, and organizational success.

However, it requires the will to ditch outdated behaviors and press the leadership development "reset" button. It's not about expecting people to fit into the current norms of the hero leader paradigm.

The Forton4D integrated model summarizes the leadership development steps as: Define, Discover, Develop and Deploy. The Forton4D model invites organizations to define the leadership need, discover the rich seam of talent that already exists, develop these people, and support them to succeed back in the workplace.

D^1: Define

The Define phase invites the organisation to pause. To stop, look around and find out what's needed in leadership terms, before leaping into development actions.

In Chapter 1, we looked at the solo leader hero myth and the need for more balanced, inclusive leadership. We explored barriers to developing a high-performing leadership culture. In this zone of discovery, we encourage questions about what kind of leadership the organization needs to be successful. It's also important to decide where to start—because it may not be with leadership development. Better teamwork or improved employee engagement may be higher priorities.

We explored how current leadership development can create win/lose relationships and undermine the whole organization. We also saw how attention to detail and better leadership matters.

Some of the counter-myths are now becoming mainstream: fewer people now believe the stereotypes, but the challenge is to reach a tipping point.

Real heroes are all around us, because they lead from where they are; let's set them free to succeed on a bigger scale.

The real challenge of the 21st century is to identify leadership skills within ourselves and support others to develop their leadership capacity too, instead of relying on single, heroic figures and defaulting to someone else's prepackaged version.

In Chapter 2, we explored different ways to define the leadership development challenge: as puzzle and problem paradigms, focusing on the new paradigm of leadership development, to meet the challenges of VUCA World.

VUCA World is created by volatility, uncertainty, complexity, and ambiguity faced by leaders. It requires a different approach to dealing with the situations they face and a new approach to leader development.

The central myth in this chapter is that the issues facing the organization today are puzzles—with "right" and "wrong" answers. In the puzzle paradigm, it takes just one hero to solve the puzzle, by following the clues. In today's world, the definitions of challenges aren't so clear; they're "problems" with no single answer.

For this, you need more than one person to address the challenge—from the perspective of their individual and collective intelligence, wisdom, and experience.

In Chapter 3, we explored why we still cling to the belief that one cape-clad hero will save the day, despite the fact that we all know it's a myth. It's time to throw off the cape and discard its underpinning beliefs, assumptions, and unconscious bias.

The new way of looking at leadership and development requires that we address four key paradigms:

The hero leader paradigm

The male over female leader paradigm

The monoculture over diversity in leadership paradigm

The older over younger leader paradigm

These paradigms, in combination, have created an *exclusive* model of leadership. When shifted, the potential exists to unlock organizational success through the better utilization of all the skills and resources available to it.

And that's what we mean by "abundant" leadership.

The paradigm needed in today's VUCA World is abundant, inclusive, engaging, flexible leadership.

We explore these dominant paradigms and the benefits, for organizations, teams, and individuals, of making change. Also under scrutiny is the notion of unconscious bias, which, along with the ego-driven heroic leader, puts up obstacles to the abundant leadership paradigm.

D^2: Discover

The discovery phase offers new ways of looking at talent selection and contests the practice of recruiting for cultural "fit," when that may not be what's needed.

In Chapter 4, we challenged the "war for talent" metaphor and argued instead for a more collaborative approach to recruitment and retention. We discovered the benefits of in-house talent nurturing versus the costs (in time and money) of hiring from outside.

The hero metaphor in this chapter is the myth of the "lone man emerging as victor," which comes from our attachment to notions of scarcity and the "finite pool" of talent, as well as the addiction to competitive methods of selection, promotion, and recruitment.

The peacemaker encourages conciliation, brings collaboration and favors negotiating, for example, by showing the common ground. The first step in the Discovery phase is to think differently and look beyond today's recruitment behaviors, by valuing and discovering the talent that already exists.

"What's the definition of an expert? Someone from a different country"

(anonymous)

In Chapter 5, we addressed the myth of the shiny suited outsider and the knight in shining armor and invited you to dig a little deeper into your talent pool. To mine for the gold that already exists in your organisation. We explored the allure of the new, and the risks. It's easy enough to see why people fall for these myths: They're enticing and seem to solve our problems in a moment.

It's not merely that organizations need to take a long hard look at what's needed; it's also vital to remove structural barriers to developing the talent you've already got.

We also looked at the notion of the wider cultural environment and how that encourages—or deters—the talent pool to step forward. And we addressed the question of when it might make sense to bring people in from outside.

In **Chapter 6,** we looked a little more closely at team composition, using the metaphor of 'filling a vase' with a range of rocks, pebbles and sand, to represent the 'stars', the managers and the day to day support skills every successful team needs.

Just as coming over as human creates bonds between people, leaders and managers don't operate in isolation from their teams. This sense of connection reduces personal feelings of loneliness and increases leaders' chances of success.

We strongly argue that leaders, especially in major turnaround situations, or when the organization needs a new cultural direction, shouldn't be left alone to deliver but should be supported by the wider organization to succeed.

In the discovery phase, there's a key myth that only the big guys matter, that it's the figurehead, rather than the team, who gets the glory. This goes to the heart of the hero myth: sucking the attention and praise, as if one person alone really does all the work. To challenge this, we offer the metaphor of filling a vase: the big rocks, pebbles, grains of sand and water together can best fill the vase. Diversity: of skills and styles, not just culture or race, is a positive benefit to organisations.

In this chapter we also explored approaches that value every member of the team for their diverse contributions, rather than the "zero sum game" of winners and losers. We discussed the need to find reward systems that align more closely to real contribution and avoid "gaming" by people looking to beat the system.

We also looked at the strengths-based approach of leadership development and three ways to encourage the environment needed for people to deliver consistently at their optimum strengths level.

D³: Develop

For development activities to be worth their investment, they need to be skills based, change behaviors and be genuinely useful in the workplace. In this section, we explore shifts in thinking about leadership development, for leaders to succeed in VUCA World.

In Chapter 7 we challenge the labeling of empathy, compassion, and collaborative skills as "soft." In today's world of work, relationships and communications between people are vital.

Emotional intelligence skills (EQ) are also integral to this environment as they enable us to handle the ambiguity of situations, the uncertainty, and the volatility. And when things go wrong, as they do in VUCA World, the learned skill of resilience helps people recover from the challenges.

The VUCA World leader is also a coach, deploying those relationship and communication skills to bring her team with her; she especially needs to understand and deploy the four themes of high-performance behaviors, specifically identified to address VUCA situations.

Developing leaders isn't just about teaching or training them, but also about peer learning. We discuss the value of facilitating this peer learning—to demonstrate the connection to the core behaviors underpinning IQ, EQ, and MQ—and then enabling colleagues to apply peer coaching. **Chapter 8** goes more deeply into the specifics of leadership behaviors and their adaptability.

Part of the challenge of the hero myth is that leadership development programs currently support that story; it's a symbiotic relationship that exists only to support the development of heroic leaders. We call this "leadership by lion taming," and we distinguish it from more practical leadership development that brings out the needed behaviors, strengths, and emotional intelligence required by today's leaders and managers.

We emphasize the less visible high-performance behaviors too, such as the everyday conversations that support and motivate team members, an essential part of the emotional intelligence cluster of behaviors.

We look at how a coachlike leader can support others to develop themselves and create a wider learning environment. We look at the benefits of tapping into people's inner values and beliefs and of delivering consistently to our strengths.

Put simply, if we believe in ourselves and see behavior as being consistent with our image of ourselves, we are more likely to apply those behaviors consistently; it's a virtuous circle.

Having talked about virtue, in **Chapter 9**, it's time to look at the shadow side. Leadership is a daily practice; a journey, not a destination. That means we practice, and sometimes fail, to be good leaders. Nobody's perfect, yet hero figures are expected to succeed, or risk being labeled as "failures."

It's vital that we address these attitudes toward failure and the fear of failure.

Doubting ourselves and others plays directly into the zero-sum "lose/lose" mentality. It's a stagnating feeling that lacks direction.

Failure paralyses and demotivates. Leadership behaviors and styles that empower are what are needed in this new paradigm.

We make a distinction between behaviors and styles. Basing our analysis on emotional intelligence models, we explore the different styles and their values, as well as their limitations.

Finally, because in VUCA World, context is everything, we look at tool selection. Leaders need to select the right tools at the right times. This might mean deploying a particular leadership style or focusing on the right competency area.

It's no good being a great orator if action is needed. And it's no good being the all-action hero and jumping into exploits if spending time thinking is a better way forward.

We've already talked about the shadow side of dealing with failure, and it's time to dismiss the notion of leaders as "better" in some way than managers, or other team members.

What we need, in VUCA World, is resourceful enablers who can motivate and inspire others and balance that need with the requirement to get the job done.

D⁴: Deploy

In Chapter 10, we support the view that the leadership skill set needs to be introduced and developed in people as early in their careers as possible.

We look at other ways of organizing leadership, such as distributing it among team members or rotating the "leadership" role. In today's flatter organization structures, this might be a new reward model—giving people the opportunity to feel fulfilled by taking on the responsibility and encouraging higher levels of humility and lower levels of ego-driven power plays.

This is deployment of support at the organizational level—by creating a positive and mature environment for leadership success.

In Chapter 11, we question whether interviews are just an expensive method for looking at people through rose-tinted spectacles. The recruitment process is an expensive one, in terms of time, money, and effort. Interviews alone don't work, and alternatives are available, including new technologies to improve the diversity of the job advertisement itself and attract a more inclusive range of qualified candidates.

Psychometrics plays a role; the belief in "objectivity" is another myth. Unconscious bias is a big term these days, and we look at ways of harnessing our understanding of unconscious perceptions, to change the recruitment environment.

Becoming conscious of our unconscious preferences is the first step to creating change in this area.

Chapter 12 explores the notion of "well-rounded people" and the desire to iron out the wrinkles, rather than accept sharp individuals who, working together, are willing to make up a well-rounded team.

The hero myth presents a character with caring traits, yet his female allies are typically killed off in the action. It's very risky to be Superman's or Spiderman's girlfriend. It's as if the late 20th century hero myth wants to "kill off" the hero's empathy outlet, yet tug at heartstrings and retain the audience's sympathy at the same time.

We need our leaders to both work at their leadership behaviors and have the character traits of emotional intelligence and flexibility in VUCA World. Most especially, we need them to build "cohesive teams" of leaders, thus increasing leadership abundance.

This calls for different leadership styles, such as a more consultative approach, in which leaders ask others for their input and contribution. It calls for a more coachlike leadership style, to really listen to people's career aspirations, which is particularly valuable when promotional options are reducing. It calls for more options, such as valuing sideways moves or using corporate social responsibility (CSR) activities to develop leaders, rather than just providing opportunities to go up an organizational ladder.

Our Conclusions

The tipping point for abundant leadership isn't going to magically happen. And if those people who have the most to lose from the shift away from solo hero leadership to a wider notion of abundance get their way, it won't happen at all.

However, younger people, women, and people of color and cultural diversity are impatient to develop. And many organizations do see the value—in financial and human terms—of abundant leadership.

The challenge is to make that change happen, to empower abundant leadership.

It's about harnessing individual responsibility with structural power; both working harmoniously together. It's about individuals and institutions aligning with the new leadership paradigm. It calls for supporting work groups such as human resources (HR), change teams, and learning and development (L&D) to work together in support of a working environment and culture that empowers leaders and managers to apply their skills. It's time to encourage and enable leaders themselves to develop the next generation of leaders, fit for the new leadership paradigms.

When those dynamics are aligned, abundant leadership will happen.

And the beauty of the interactive, digital, and social world in which we now live means that even the solo child walking out of her school to call for change isn't really alone. She is supported by the power of social media. So even that one person is a part of the more connected, abundant leadership whole.

About the Authors

Bob Hughes is a leadership consultant, co-founder of the UK-based Forton Group, who designs and delivers leadership development globally, coaching board members and senior leaders, including using the my360plus leadership assessment tool. Co-creator of the internationally accredited "Leadership Coaching Model," his expertise is built on 30 years' working in major corporates at a senior level. He is  also a nonexecutive director for Engage for Success, which promotes employee engagement to benefit individuals, teams, and organizations.

Helen Caton Hughes is an international author, leadership coach, researcher, and learning and development program design consultant. Co-founder of the Forton Group, Helen works with leaders internationally to create and deliver engaging leadership development programs that apply the practical tools relevant to 21st-century leadership. Her expertise is based on a corporate background includ-  ing financial services, facilities management, and marketing organizations. Her research interests include well-being in the workplace, employee engagement, volunteering, and learning design.

Index

OTHER TITLES IN THE HUMAN RESOURCE MANAGEMENT AND ORGANIZATIONAL BEHAVIOR COLLECTION

- *Comparative Management Studies* by Alan S. Gutterman
- *Breakthrough: Career Strategies for Women's Success* by Saundra Stroope
- *Women Leaders: The Power of Working Abroad* by Sapna Welsh and Caroline Kersten
- *Practicing Leadership* by Alan S. Gutterman
- *Practicing Management* by Alan S. Gutterman
- *Temperatism, Volume II: Doing Good Through Business With a Social Conscience* by Carrie Foster
- *What Millennials Really Want From Work and Life* by Yuri Kruman
- *The Generation Myth: How to Improve Intergenerational Relationships in the Workplace* by Michael J. Urick
- *Virtual Vic: A Management Fable* by Laurence M. Rose
- *Our Glassrooms: Perceptiveness and Its Implications for Transformational Leadership* by Dhruva Trivedy
- *The New World of Human Resources and Employment: How Artificial Intelligence and Process Redesign is Driving Dramatic Change* by Tony Miller
- *From Behind the Desk to the Front of the Stage: How to Enhance Your Presentation Skills* by David Worsfold
- *No Dumbing Down: A No-Nonsense Guide for CEOs on Organization Growth* by Karen D. Walker
- *Redefining Competency Based Education: Competence for Life* by Nina Morel and Bruce Griffiths
- *Skilling India: Challenges and Opportunities* by S. Nayana Tara and Sanath Kumar
- *Creating a Successful Consulting Practice* by Gary W. Randazzo
- *How Successful Engineers Become Great Business Leaders* by Paul Rulkens

Announcing the Business Expert Press Digital Library

Concise e-books business students need for classroom and research

This book can also be purchased in an e-book collection by your library as

- *a one-time purchase,*
- *that is owned forever,*
- *allows for simultaneous readers,*
- *has no restrictions on printing, and*
- *can be downloaded as PDFs from within the library community.*

Our digital library collections are a great solution to beat the rising cost of textbooks. E-books can be loaded into their course management systems or onto students' e-book readers. The **Business Expert Press** digital libraries are very affordable, with no obligation to buy in future years. For more information, please visit **www.businessexpertpress.com/librarians**. To set up a trial in the United States, please email **sales@businessexpertpress.com**.

Lightning Source UK Ltd.
Milton Keynes UK
UKHW020654220419
341361UK00004B/64/P